Astro Power

**A simple guide
to prediction and destiny,
for the modern mystic**

Vanessa Montgomery

Hardie Grant

QUADRILLE

Harnessing astro power p.4

I.

Studying astrological transits p.6

II.

Cycles p.18

III.

Fundamentals p.36

IV.

The planets p.60

V.

Putting it all together p.202

Harnessing astro power

Making meaning out of what seems like chaos in these 'uncertain times' continues to drive interest in astrology, which is well designed to deliver answers. We all want to know what's around the corner – now more than ever – and, more importantly, how to shape our own destiny. Many consumers are now aware of the basics of astrology and the cosmic universe and want to delve a little deeper into how they can benefit from this understanding in a way that is still approachable and accessible.

The fact is, life is full of surprises and always has been, which is why predictive astrological timing techniques and a range of divinatory oracles have persisted through millennia. Today, astro-curiosity ranges from reading the daily Sun sign horoscope to webinars on Saturn's return or headlines on cosmic alignment.

These are all based on the movement of planets, the Sun signs and astrological houses they are in, and the aspects – or angles – they make to one another. That is the focus of this handbook. It will help you to understand the essential meaning of each planet, how it relates to all the other planets, and how the whole structure fits together. With this astro-powered knowledge at your disposal, you'll understand which factors experts and the media use when discussing the next Mercury retrograde or the year ahead. You'll know what it means for you personally rather than a one-size-fits-all interpretation that doesn't seem to relate to you. It will give you the knowledge to enable you to separate clickbait hype from what to pay attention to as you navigate towards your destiny.

What's more, tracking the planets and Moon in real time gets us away from our screens and encourages us to engage with the beautiful natural world around us. We can literally see the Sun rise and set every day, note the changes in the Moon over the course of the month and spot Venus (the brightest planet in the sky) from where we stand on Earth. I don't know about you, but when I look up at the Moon and stars I feel my energy shift, my body relax, and I'm able to breathe deeply. It's essential for our physical and mental wellbeing to tune into our environment, encourage our symbolic mind and connect with others in meaningful ways. I do believe astrology is a great tool to do so.

Use this book to understand your cyclical evolution, predict the outcome of crises and plan ahead to make the most of particularly favourable periods. Discover when cosmic times in your life will begin and end, and what you can do to get the most out of them. Understand which archetypal themes are at play, which areas, moods or industries will rise and fall, and work out the best times to go for something, or when to be patient yet persistent when challenges arise.

Most importantly, this book will be fun! It's thrilling to be able to tap into the cosmic universe to see what life has in store for you, and how you can adapt and change within various transits, time periods or Moon phases to get the most out of life and avoid missing out.

Think of this book as your personal cosmic calendar and make the most of every opportunity that the universe sends your way. As with my first two books, *Astro Power* reloads astrology for the modern mystic through language and metaphor that is empowering, uplifting and focuses on female and non-binary experiences. This book, in particular, will touch on the themes of identity, individual potential and prediction.

Although there are many predictive techniques, the skill you are about to learn is the first and most fundamental one used to understand any date or period in the past, present or future, either from the point of view of the individual or society as a whole. It is referred to as astrological transits, or simply, transits.

I.

Studying astrological transits

What are transits and how can we use them to better understand our destiny? Quite simply, transit means in transition; it reflects that something is either changing, ready to change or needs to change in your life.

A planet transiting means it's moving. It could be:
- Moving through a sign, its element and mode
- Passing into a sign or out of a sign
- At a particular angle with another planet; an aspect
- Making an aspect or connection with a particular point on your birth chart
- Moving through an astrological house

Two levels of transit

In this book, you'll learn about transits on two levels. The first reflects the collective: like why a decade has a particular theme and the archetype underlying major trends. It's the astro-weather or picking up on the collective world soul.

The second level is how transits relate to you personally, and how to plan and respond so that you are in tune with the astro energies. This book includes a refresher on the essential components that form the basis of horoscopic astrology and the transits. Then, we'll dive into the planets and their meanings when in transit.

Standing the test of time

Although astrology has developed over millennia, the form we're familiar with today began to take shape in Ancient Babylon c.1800BC. From there, moving through to Greek Alexandria, it combined with Egyptian astronomical cosmology, and was organized into a twelve-house, twelve-sign horoscope by the order-loving Greeks.

Ancient Greece rebranded with deities from their pantheon, Rome renamed them, later passing on the cosmic system to Islamic and Jewish astrologers who continued to develop it over time. Europe during the Middle Ages saw astrology taught as a scholarly university subject, with doctors having to consult the stars by law before procedures. Dropping out by the 18th century, astrology had an on/off relationship with the Christian church. Astrology as a utility suggests the individual can connect directly with the cosmos rather than through a priest as an intermediary channel.

You're in fine company

With a lineage that includes famous names who worked in multi-disciplinary times with titles incorporating, but not limited to, scholar-astrologer-astronomer-mathemetician-philosopher-priest/ priestess-magi-alchemist-geographer-cosmologist-physicist-physician, you're in good company. Famous proponents who feature in astrology's stellar past include:

- Ptolemy, 2nd century
- Hypatia, 4th century
- Nostradamus, 16th century
- Copernicus, 16th century
- Galileo, 17th century
- Kepler, 17th century
- Evangeline Adams, 20th century
- Carl Jung, 20th century

The cosmic calendar and how it works

Astrology's framework is built on the planets' dependable, observable and trackable circuits from our vantage point here on Earth. Each time a planet moves into a sign or a particular alignment with another planet, it's like the hands on a celestial clock chiming the hour, indicating that you are psychologically ready to develop, move or change. Encounters that provide challenge, a stroke of luck, a curve in career or a relationship are all on the menu, depending on what a configuration represents. Through understanding the transits, you can be ready to make that change, take that leap and grow, or resist and suffer the inner tension or watch missed opportunity phase out like the lunar cycle. Essentially, you can understand themes around past events and relate them to the future.

Like Alice through the looking glass, it's through this mechanistic framework that the archetypal, intuitive and symbolic components of astrology are accessed. Once you feed the rational, conscious part of your mind the left-brain style of data it likes, your symbolic, intuitive right brain can pick up on relevant themes and potential outcomes. Astrology is multivalent; there are many possible expressions within its motifs and archetypes. This is where your intuitive or mystic side can jump through the framework you've learnt and pick up on what resonates with you. No pressure; if you stick to the book, keywords and themes, you're still going to find your way.

Fate, destiny and free will

Understanding the concepts of fate, destiny and free will is essential in this context, so it is important to identify your beliefs. We are all constrained in different ways by our material circumstances, laws and the society in which we live. However, astrology suggests certain predispositions, and that there exists a wide arc of fate in which we exercise free will and make our own choices on how to express, handle or respond to cosmic timing.

Do you have an inner locus of control, or is it external? Do you believe the gods, fate, destiny or someone else dictates your life – an external locus? Or do you believe you have complete responsibility and control over your choices – an internal locus? Where on the spectrum are you? If you find you are avoiding decisions, waiting for validation or permission to take action, perhaps it is time to revisit those principles. Likewise if you feel too responsible for a situation that may be culturally systemic or truly beyond your control, revisit and review. Be aware if you are too passive and not taking action. Or too rational, not receptive or ignoring the intuitive flow, perhaps not recognizing the messages from your alternative channels of intel. Bring awareness to your operating system so you can commandeer your destiny.

Mercury made me do it – correlation versus causality

In this book, I refer to correlations, not causality. The idea that a celestial object causes something in your life (external locus of control) may be a way of not taking responsibility or leave you feeling like a victim to fate or circumstance.

As iconic psychologist Carl Jung proposed with his theory of synchronicity, a correlation, correspondence or meaningful coincidence, on the other hand, is empowering and encourages your active participation. It leaves room for choice and response while fostering a deep relationship and trust with your innate intelligence and inner knowing. The 'as above, so below' principle suggests we are plugged into a cosmic intelligence; we are part of and an essential expression of it. This is not a religious view but is certainly a mystic one that will add depth to your astrology practice.

This too shall pass – hang in there!

If you're having a tough time, aren't relating to the world or it looks like gnarly transits are coming up, the cyclical nature of astrology promises that this too shall pass. There may be a bunch of planets in signs that you just don't vibe with, but when they come around to signs and positions that do, it will be your time to shine! Hang in there, make the most of the call to arms, be patient and ride it out. The same may be said for those times when you are riding the crest of the wave. Make the most of it and don't take it for granted! The traction you gain over this period will help you cruise through lean times.

Ego, projection, transits and modern psychology

As I use it in this book, the term 'ego' is a concept of self, of identity: a collection of ideas or feelings about oneself that we use as an operating platform or interface with the world. This part of ourselves has its place and role, partly to keep us alive. We may fight to keep our identity or protect it from anything we perceive as a threat or which can impede growth. It's essential to foster a healthy ego but not let it run the entire show.

Challenging transits may represent a time when it's difficult to integrate two parts of yourself that seem at odds or have very different needs, roles or functions. The ego may identify with one part and project the other onto an external situation or person. The part of the self that we see as acceptable is owned, while the part that we can't own is projected. This is often called the shadow, or sometimes the golden shadow. Knowing the themes represented by both planets involved in the transit will identify which parts of yourself or life are clashing and need either separate expression or simply to be accepted as part of the whole you.

Astro Power

Archetypes

Jung, who used astrology in his professional practice, said 'astrology represents the sum of all the psychological knowledge of antiquity' and so has much to offer.

Archetypes are universal patterns of expression that repeat and are recognizable: like the mother, the parent, the trickster. We see them in myth, dreams and compelling stories. They are also expressed through the planets and signs in astrology.

Myths and stories link us through images to our unconscious and symbolic mind. They tap into the creative potency of imagination. A mytho-poetic way of looking at the archetypes represented in astrology allows us to recognize them and helps us define something calling for expression. Perhaps that is a part of our nature that doesn't have a way of being understood or accepted in today's reductive, mechanistic, rational world view. Archetypes enable us to see beyond personality and the surface level of ego awareness into underlying issues at play, recognize them in others as well as in interpersonal and collective dynamics. Story writers and movie makers use classic archetypes – like the protagonist's journey, the mentor and the tempter – because we all recognize and relate to them. Unfortunately, advertising uses them as well!

Ancient Greek and Roman archetypes

Times change and we change with them. We play an active role in progressing them by being the change, pushing the needle forward through leadership, representation, influence and cold, hard legislation. Western astrology, like our culture, has a lot to thank Ancient Greece and Rome for. However, that extremely repressive patriarchy casts a long shadow onto today, with imbalanced gender concepts still used to describe planets and signs in astrology, among other things. Do as the Greco-Romans did: rebrand! Take the best and cast the rest in your own image.

The Ancient Greco-Roman pantheon of goddesses and gods partially informs archetypes in astrology, but not entirely. The archetypes Ancient mythology are wrapped around are timeless and helpful to understand. However, the cultural cloak they wear needs an update or we're perpetuating a repressive binary with an arbitrary division down a gender line. It's crucial to remember that other cultures in the region were more egalitarian, while preceding ones had a radically different social structure and cosmology.

Crete, by all accounts, was egalitarian, while the Etruscans and Spartans enjoyed civil rights, education and a lot of freedom for women. The flip side was in Ancient Athens, where women's lives have been compared to the worst of those living under the Taliban. They were property, not considered citizens and malnourished on half rations. It's a bit depressing when you see that, in earlier cultures, women had been revered, represented in mythology as the supreme deity, but had subsequently disappeared from stories of respect to social inferiority. If the genders in the Greco-Roman stories were flipped, there would be outrage and backlash, as there often is now when we bust out of our lanes. It wasn't always like that and doesn't need to be now.

The new school

Be aware of which myths you tell, use or revisit to illustrate concepts through your astrology. By understanding the archetypal themes, you can share them through a new story or image that's timeless yet modern and empowering to you and your diverse audience.

Planets and signs have been seen as male or female or non-binary, like Mercury or Uranus. However, they don't have gender, just as traits like strength, thought or emotional needs belong to everyone, regardless. Let's continue to liberate ourselves and others by mixing it up or using non-gendered terms. Diversity in astrology is as essential as in the workplace. You've got to see it to be it, so help yourself by revisioning and opening up what's possible. The planets, signs and houses in astrology represent parts of ourselves no matter who we are or our identity. It's the great leveller in many ways as we all share these common qualities.

Self-realization

Why is this important? Remember transit means a time of transition and change. Suppose you are in a position where you want to open the idea of yourself to more. That may require stepping out of a limited, socially enforced lane to allow yourself to blossom towards a fuller realization of yourself and your destiny.

If the old school tells you Saturn is a patriarchal figure or the Sun is a male/masculine or a king, but you are female or ditching the gender binary altogether, just use the qualities, not the gender, as they are what matters. The same goes for outdated notions of superiority around ethnic, cultural or socio-economic backgrounds. Our warrior archetype, Mars, may be any brave soul. The active, athletic and sometimes aggressive qualities the traditional Mars represents don't have to be culturally coded; with a modern perspective, we can discard the gender stereotyping. Old-fashioned socialized or cultural limitations should be thrown out. Instead, use the qualities relevant to you and author your own story. Light the way for others by expressing your vision in a new language! The transiting planets activating your natal planet positions will indicate when you're chafing at the bit to bust out!

Calculating a birth chart

The core of your study is going to be the astrological chart. The most common is your birth chart, but you can also do charts for other snapshots in time: for an event, for a country or for the particular time of a transit.

Birth charts

You can calculate your own birth chart or have one done for you (see overleaf). Your birth, or natal, chart is a map of the heavens at the time of your birth, so ideally you need the date, place and time you were born. It shows you your Sun sign and the positions of all the planets in the zodiac signs at the time of your birth. The chart is usually rendered in both list and diagrammatic form. From this, it will calculate the aspects, or angles, forming between each of the planets. Specific aspects – square, trine, conjunction, sextiles and opposition – have different effects and we will go into more detail on that in later chapters.

Print out your birth chart and make sure you understand the positions of the planets on the horoscope circle. Then you are equipped to start to interpret the information.

Location horoscopes

Similarly, you can have a horoscope drawn up on the websites listed at the end of this book for any time, day and place. You could choose the time of an important event in your own life, or a historical event that you wish to examine. You can also compare that data with what is in the stars in the future.

Countries have a horoscope, as do cities. Search your country on the internet and you'll find plenty about its astrology. You can watch the transits for your country and begin to predict how those transits transpire based on history and the current situation. What is your country's Sun, Moon and rising sign?

Where to get your charts

You can calculate your birth chart for free at **astro.com**, my website **astroallstarz.com** or invest in the app **astrogold.io**. The astro gold app will be the easiest to use as it will display the double-ringed horoscope of your birth chart, or any time you choose, circled by the current transits. It will also give you a mini suggestion of what each individual placement means, which will get you started. It's a one-time payment. Another option is **LUNAastrology.com**, which is a great budget-friendly option based on subscription.

For those who are getting the hang of things, going the old-fashioned way means consulting an ephemeris, such as the *New International Ephemerides 1900–2050*, or finding a digital version online at **astro.com**. From these tables of figures, you can draw up your own charts by hand.

Example birth chart of…

Charley, born
September 16, 1997
at 9:55pm in
Sydney, Australia

♈	Aries	☉	Sun
♉	Taurus	☽	Moon
♊	Gemini	☿	Mercury
♋	Cancer	♀	Venus
♌	Leo	♂	Mars
♍	Virgo	♃	Jupiter
♎	Libra	♄	Saturn
♏	Scorpio	⚷	Chiron
♐	Sagittarius	♅	Uranus
♑	Capricorn	♆	Neptune
♒	Aquarius	♇	Pluto
♓	Pisces	☊	North Node
		☋	South Node

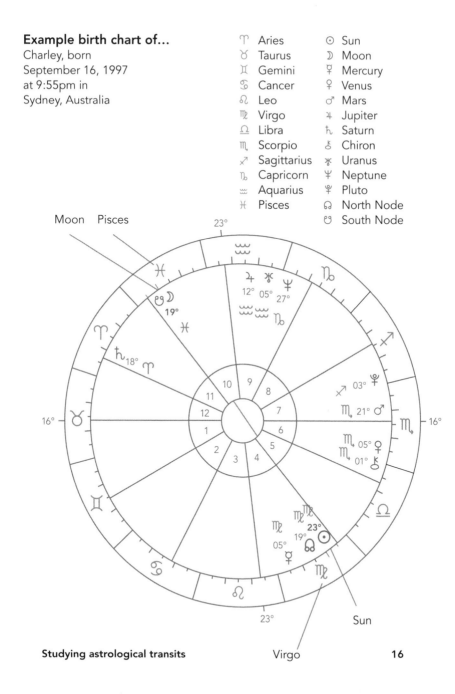

Start your own astrological notes

Now is a good time to open a folder or start a notebook – digital or physical – to keep all your research and the knowledge you gain as you go through this book.

You could start with a vision board for each planet and sign, or one that expresses yourself as each archetype. What would you look and feel like as Mars? How would you enter a room, speak, hold yourself? How would you act in a particular situation? Be aware of your feelings around that. Note any excitement or resistance and reflect on what your body and mind are telling you to help you navigate through it and expand what is possible for you. You might want to repeat the exercise after a time and see if your ideas of self have changed. As you work your way through the text, make sure you understand each phase before moving on.

You can make other visual collages, too, to show the energies you are discovering. Images can often encapsulate concepts or feelings more easily than words.

Don't limit your study to images – take notes and file the components logically to make them easy to refer to. Be imaginative and record any areas that you think are interesting or worth further reflection. Remember to record what you are thinking and feeling.

You might also like to begin a timeline of your life, allowing plenty of space to keep adding and developing information. Mark particular milestones – starting school or university, career shifts, changes in your personal life – so you can gradually examine the prevailing astrological influences at the time and whether you were making the most of them or whether you could do better next time.

Some people like to study alone, while others prefer to learn in groups. You may like to find a friend, start a group or get into forums to practise your new language if you learn well that way. Remember, though, that astrology is a highly symbolic language that can incorporate a huge breadth of information in one symbol or glyph alone, so be patient with yourself as you learn and apply your skills.

Above all, practise, practise, practise – there is no substitute.

II.

Cycles

If there's one thing we learn from astrology it's that life isn't exactly linear. While they orbit around the central organizing principle of our solar system, our Sun, the planets are constantly spinning on their axes. This compelling cyclical component was built into the Ancient spiritually infused understanding of life. It's a spiral of evolution; we continue from where we left off rather than beginning again at point zero.

This chapter recaps the foundation you'll need for understanding and forecasting with transits. Use it to gain knowledge if this is not all familiar and build your note folder as you go. If you are familiar with the content, it will act as a refresher or guide to check back. There are a lot of moving parts in the astrological cosmic code, so making your lists and notes will help you file and remember them in a logical sequence.

Planetary cycles

Each planet circles constantly through all twelve signs of the zodiac. Each one makes its rounds in its own time depending on how close to, or how far from, the Sun it is. These cycles underpin this book for understanding various points in history and for looking ahead to the future.

Taking a snapshot of any one planet at any one moment is useful, but it exists within a larger system, as do we. However, it's a place to begin, especially when you're learning. Focus in on one thread, then add it in context to other cycles, and the mix of signs and aspects at that time.

The personal versus the collective destiny

Looking at transits is particularly interesting as the influence of planetary transits has an effect on the long-term trends of both the collective and the individual. Keep in mind throughout this book that I'll be toggling between both levels.

The collective transits refer to planets in signs and in relationship to each other. Making it personal means overlaying the transiting planets onto your birth chart. This goes a long way to explaining why people may thrive better than others at various points in their lives. The transiting planets of the times are locking into your chart in a different way from theirs (unless you were born at exactly the same date, place and time). It's a good reminder not to compare your life to anyone else's and to respect that each of you has a unique journey.

Astro Power

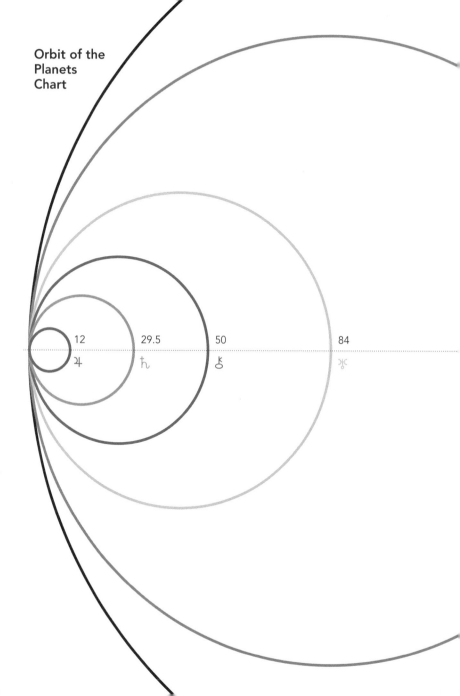

Orbit of the
Planets
Chart

12 ♃

29.5 ♄

50 ♌

84 ♅

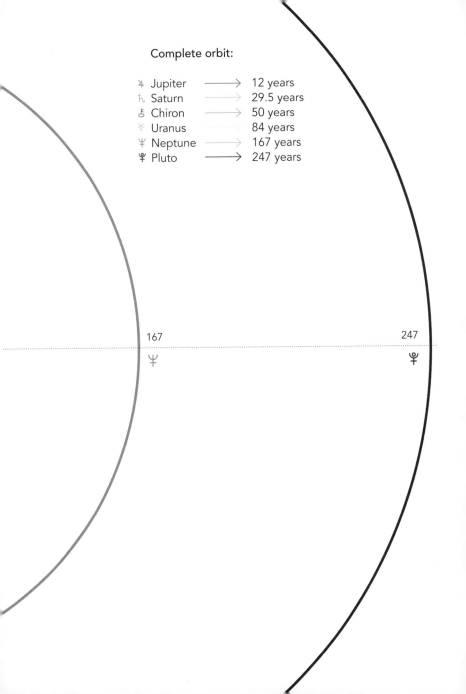

Complete orbit:

♃ Jupiter $\longrightarrow$ 12 years
♄ Saturn $\longrightarrow$ 29.5 years
⚷ Chiron $\longrightarrow$ 50 years
♅ Uranus 84 years
♆ Neptune $\longrightarrow$ 167 years
♇ Pluto $\longrightarrow$ 247 years

167
♆

247
♇

Your generation

There are things a generation is destined to deal with, impact and evolve. It's like a group destiny: you meet as a collective. If you were born at the beginning of the sign, you are well positioned to be a leader, to watch for the signs of change and be the first to ride the wave. People born when a planet is further into a sign will see the themes taking shape around them. When you're young you might think it has always been this way. As you go through the years and those planets change signs, you'll see the themes change with the new generation and see yours with more objectivity. This is where most people experience the generation gap and some resist the mission of the next generation simply because it's different from their own. Understanding this part of astrology goes a long way to help you to embrace and make the most of what each generation has to offer.

The online engagement between the millennial generations and the baby boomers is a case in point. Astrologically, millennials have Pluto in Scorpio, which sits in a tense square aspect to the boomer generation's Pluto in Leo. As you'll understand more fully as we go through the book, they just don't see eye to eye.

Check out which combination of sub-generation you belong to and consult your birth chart to see where these outer planets are positioned. Where are they transiting in relation to your birth chart at this moment? Make notes in your file.

Reflect on the big collective trends and movements of the time you were born into. You carry this energy with you like a seed. As you grow through life, you and your generation are here to bring these themes to fruition.

The sign of the times
– the outer planets

The further out from the Sun a planet is, the slower its orbit and therefore the longer it spends in each sign. This means it has greater correlation to what we experience as a collective theme in history and what we remember about that time. The slow-moving outer planets of Uranus, Neptune and Pluto have much to say about the bigger picture for a whole generation because they are in a single sign for so long that individuals share this placement with everyone born within several years.

Once you know the themes of each planet and of the host sign, you can predict what's coming up. Look at what happened the last time a particular planet was in a particular sign and you will see a pattern emerging.

It's easy to look ahead at which sign these planets will be in and when. The sign will tell you which areas will come into popular consciousness. Learn the themes of each planet and sign, then put the combo together. Always look back for clues going forward. And remember the signs will already be forming if you're willing to notice and jump on board early. The astrology will confirm which threads will take hold and dominate.

Neptune

For example, Neptune tells us the spirit of the times. Its 14-year transit through a sign means an entire decade and then some will be stamped with its signature themes. Since Neptune shows up visually in arts and spiritual trends, it's easy to identify. The swinging sixties were all about sexual revolution, and Neptune was in potent and provocative Scorpio. Waistlines dropped to the hips, emphasizing the pelvic region, which happens to be the area of the body ruled by Scorpio.

In the 1970s, Neptune was in exotica-loving, globe-trotting Sagittarius. The West embraced Eastern spirituality and proportion became exaggerated: those bell bottom flares, big glasses, hairstyles and platform shoes.

In early 2012, Neptune moved into Pisces. Over this period, we saw a renewed interest in modern mysticism, tarot, astrology, crystals and compassion through veganism. It will be remembered for all these things and the colour to rule them all, millennial pink. Once Neptune moves into assertive Aries, the vibe and cultural wallpaper will look vastly different while dreamy pink may turn to high-energy red.

Uranus

Uranus correlates with progress in exciting and novel technology as it reaches the masses, changing the landscape. In early 2018, Uranus entered Taurus, so we knew in advance there would be disruption (Uranus) and interest in Taurus-ruled areas. So far, among other things, we see cryptocurrency and fintech, plants and nature are trending, and meat is being grown in labs. Previously in me-me-me Aries, fitness, activewear and selfies became a thing.

The synodic cycle – it takes two

A synodic cycle is the cycle two planets make in relation to each other. It begins when they meet in a conjunction. The faster of the pair will move into aspects we know as the first (opening or waxing) square, the opposition and so on until it eventually catches up with the slower-moving planet, meeting once again and beginning a new cycle.

The themes of those two planets correlate to events we experience in our culture. When more than one planet convenes in any one sign, the themes of that sign are even more pronounced.

Jupiter and Saturn

An example is the Jupiter and Saturn cycle. Ancient astrologers named this cycle the monarch-maker since its 20-year synodic cycle was about the lifespan of a ruler. It was used to predict the end of a ruling power and the coming of a new one. We can expect a change in the nature of rulership, among other things.

The planets meet up every 20 years for 200 years in signs of a particular element. When they begin a new 200-year cycle in the next element, it is called the great mutation. We've just begun a new 200-year cycle in Air, after 200 years in the Earth element. That happens to correlate with the industrial revolution. Things were built; it was tangible. The Air cycle already looks to correlate with a move into virtual worlds, the commodification of information and attention, and in China, a social credit system (Air is the social principle). The last time Jupiter and Saturn moved through Air signs, the printing press and paper made information accessible to more people than hand-copied manuscripts onto vellum. The Silk Road was in full swing. What is now China has begun opening and extending in the one-belt one-road initiative. Looking back will always give us clues and allow us to verify the themes forming around us and the direction they may take.

The last Jupiter–Saturn conjunction in late 2020 was in Aquarius, so perhaps Aquarian themes will show up around who rules, and how. This may be through technology, science, the group over the individual and humanitarian concerns. When Jupiter moves to oppose Saturn, that rulership may face some opposition or it could be the peak of that cycle.

The Berlin Wall went up when Jupiter and Saturn were conjunct (beginning a new cycle) in Capricorn (Capricorn themes, especially paired with Saturn, can be restriction and control). For East Germany, the new ruler was the Soviet Union. The wall was up for 30 years, which is one and a half cycles (and one return of Saturn) so when it came down, Jupiter (and Chiron) was opposite Saturn and indeed there was opposition, which thankfully won the day.

The more planets involved in close or exact aspects, the more the energies suggest a big event is likely, relative to what happened earlier in the cycle. It's an evolution of the theme or story. In some ways it's like the s/hero's journey but this is the journey of the collective rather than the individual.

Saturn and Uranus

When pairing Saturn with Uranus, Saturn is the faster-moving planet, taking the lead and moving first into each aspect. Since Saturn rules established systems like the government, where Uranus rules progress, technology and sudden destabilizing events, this cycle tends to see the people go head to head with restrictive government – and that government attempting to restrict! These planets, along with Neptune (dissolution and oneness) in a triple conjunction were in opposition to Jupiter when the Berlin Wall fell. Saturn in Capricorn was in its sign of rulership representing tangible boundaries. A year before, Saturn and Uranus had met up in freedom-themed Sagittarius, perhaps setting the scene for the following year's events. While East Germans flooding through to the West happened suddenly, change had come on the back of revolutions that had been taking place with smaller countries splintering off the USSR, bearing themes of Uranian revolution and impactful change.

Synodic cycles at a glance

This is the time it takes from one conjunction to the next. List when the two transiting planets formed major aspects. Look back at headlines in history and compare it to the cycle they're in now. When did they last meet up, and when is the next conjunction?

Jupiter/Saturn: 20 years
Jupiter/Uranus: 14 years
Jupiter/Neptune: 13 years
Jupiter/Pluto: 12 years
Saturn/Uranus: 45 years
Saturn/Neptune: 35–36 years
Saturn/Pluto: 34–35 years
Uranus/Neptune: 170 years
Uranus/Pluto: 140 years
Neptune/Pluto: 500 years

Saturn returns and other milestones

Saturn return means Saturn has moved from the place it was when you were born, made a full orbit and is back to that exact place. If you overlay the transit chart over your birth chart (see page 207), Saturn will be sitting right on top of your natal Saturn and you'll be 29.5 years old if this is your first Saturn return. These types of milestone transits are known as the generic cycle. They refer to the transiting planet's relationship to its position in your natal chart. Everyone has most of them at the same age and they coincide with developmental milestones.

No doubt you have experienced the terrible twos or at least seen them in action in the supermarket! At two years old, we all experience our first Mars return since it has a two-year orbit. The toddler is expressing Mars, pushing boundaries, saying NO, basically trying it on and saying 'my way' or I'll explode in anger and rage (Mars attacks)! They push back!

Another example is the mid-life crisis which is marked by transiting Uranus opposite natal Uranus at around the age of 41. The destabilizing time for change is here. Do you pivot into your next phase or do you cling to your thirties, quit your job and buy a red sports car (or a bit of both)?! Although there are more milestones than in the illustrated timeline (overleaf), these are the major milestone transits and ages at which they occur. Check the planets section to learn more.

Defining Milestones Chart

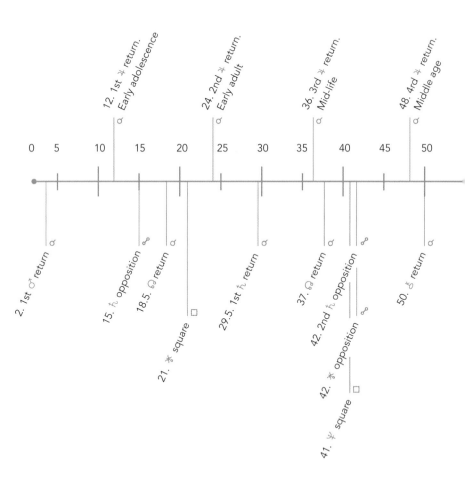

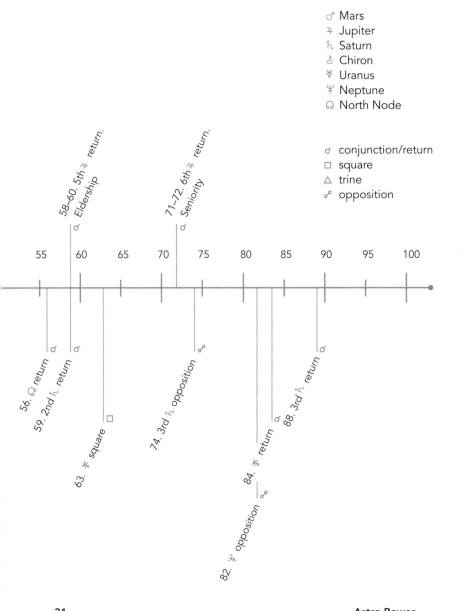

♂ Mars
♃ Jupiter
♄ Saturn
⚷ Chiron
♅ Uranus
♆ Neptune
☊ North Node

♂ conjunction/return
□ square
△ trine
☍ opposition

58–60. 5th ♃ return.
Eldership
σ

71–72. 6th ♃ return.
Seniority
σ

55 60 65 70 75 80 85 90 95 100

56. ☊ return
σ
59. 2nd ♄ return
σ

74. 3rd ♄ opposition
☍

84. ♅ return
σ
88. 3rd ♄ return
σ

63. ♅ square
□

82. ♆ opposition
☍

Astro Power

Retrograde and retro-shade

You usually hear retrograde talked about in terms of Mercury, but all planets retrograde except the Sun and Moon (although they are technically not planets but luminaries).

Astronomically a planet going retrograde is just an optical illusion, just as when you are on a train and pass another, it looks as though it is moving backwards. From our perspective here on Earth, as we cycle around the Sun, when a planet that moves at a different rate to Earth either passes us, or we pass it, we perceive it as a retrograde.

The distance between the Earth and planet in question sets the duration of the retrograde. The closer the planet to Earth, the shorter the retrograde. Mercury spends the least time in a back spin while Pluto averages the most. In a nutshell, the three re's define the retrograde period: re-flect, re-visit, re-do. Assess and make a course correction, if necessary.

There are three main stages in the retrograde cycle:

1. Pre-retro-shade

This is the area (the degrees) the planet will be backtracking during the retrograde. This is the set up or opening scene. It's the first pass or, if you were in a car, the initial drive by.

2. Retrograde

Before a planet retrogrades back over that slice of the zodiac it just covered, it slows down. Mercury moves quickly so it's more of a pivot, while the outer planets tend to grind down those gears to a snail's pace. This is called 'stationing'. If it's still creeping along, it's 'stationing direct'. As soon as it turns, it's called 'stationing retrograde'. The planet appears to stall at that particular degree, then very slowly begins to trace back through the degrees it has already passed through, while picking up pace. This is where the main event happens if there is going to be one. For example, you drop your phone while writing a text and press send as you pick it up, then realize you've sent the text to the wrong person... or you just realize you shouldn't have cut that corner and now have to go back and attend to what you knew you should have done in the first place. Retrogrades are useful in our fast-paced world. They make sure you loop back and deal with situations that you might otherwise not resolve, like reversing back down a road to pick up something you forgot but need, like your phone or wallet.

3. Post-retro-shade

Technically known as 'in shadow', this time the planet slows down, 'stationing retrograde', then 'stationing direct' from where it picks up pace as it moves forward. It's finally clear of retro-shade once it passes the original degree it began the retrograde from. This is like driving back down the road once again heading to your original destination.

The entire retrograde period is over once the planet clears the point at which it began the retrograde.

Being aware of retrograde

Take note of the degree a planet begins its retrograde from, and the degree it backtracks to. Note the sign it is in, the house in your natal chart and any natal planets it will contact. Some retrogrades won't count for much and some will; it depends on what kind of contacts the planet makes in your birth chart.

Finally, note that some planets retrograde frequently, so one planet or point in your chart may be in a close aspect up to five times. It's like that driver who just keeps backing up and running over the same pain or opportunity point. Check ahead for major transits so you're not taken by surprise by that second reverse or third direct drive by; you get another round to get it right, or another shot at lady luck if it's a fortuitous transit.

Mercury retrograde

Much maligned, we've all heard of Mercury retrograde. But is it all hype?

Interestingly, the etymology of disaster meant an ill-starred omen or event. Ancients believed that when a star was in an unfavourable position, events would reflect that disharmony. This doesn't just apply to retrogrades, it may be a set of challenging aspects between planets.

A positive framing comes from Rockefeller with this take on plans going awry. 'I always try to turn every disaster into an opportunity.'

Two of the best-known disasters in modern history occurred while Mercury was retrograde. The so-called 'unsinkable' Titanic sank to the bottom of the ocean. The explosion of the Hindenburg Zeppelin spelled the end for gas-filled airship aviation. These are extreme examples, so not directly relevant to day-to-day life for most people. They also demonstrate that human faults are far more likely to have caused the disasters. The Titanic carried far too few lifeboats for the number of people on board: a clear illustration of hubris over preparedness. As for the Hindenburg, quitting while ahead would have been wise after so many prior Zeppelin explosions. The lesson? Slow down and don't tempt fate! Take time out of regular programming to circle back.

Planets out of bounds of the Sun (OOB)

This is an intermediate extra but it's an interesting phenomenon. When a planet is OOB, it's out of the bounds of the Sun's highest point at midsummer and lowest point at midwinter. You'll need a declination ephemeris or list to check the declination, but you'll be looking for anything from 23° 28' since the Sun only makes it to 23° 27' north or south at the summer and winter solstices. CafeAstrology.com features an OOBs dates table.

When a planet is out of bounds of the Sun, central control no longer has jurisdiction. These planets may be untethered from social expectation or norms; they may be more creative, act independently or simply not be concerned with the usual status quo. At these times we may not follow the rules, which is great if you're a creative like Lady Gaga, who has Mars out of bounds natally, but perhaps not if you're ignoring your credit limit.

The Sun represents identity, the self and conscious awareness, so this could be a time when you act out of character. Since Christmas and light festivals generally fall over the Sagittarius and Capricorn season, planets are often OOB in these signs, which may add to those extra-wild parties, spending or indulging. You may look back and question what you were thinking, so check for transiting planets out of bounds and run extreme plans by a sensible friend before you run into trouble.

III.

Fundamentals

This section covers all the fundamental information you need to know so that you develop a real understanding of astro power. These fundamentals and how they interact are crucial to interpreting transit astrology:

- Zodiac signs
- Elements
- Modes
- Aspects
- Houses or temples

In general charts or individual birth charts, each of these units acts according to its specific nature. Each piece of the code is what it is and relentlessly expresses its nature. When Uranus comes along, it will do its liberation dance all over a sector of your life, so you may as well harness it and ride the winds of destiny!

Constructing the data

These pieces of cosmic code all have a part to play in your astrological knowledge. Start with one of the fundamentals, then overlay the remaining issues for further depth of knowledge. Some people prefer to combine signs and elements, then add modes, aspects and houses; others start with planets, others with aspects – see which works better for you.

If you're interpreting how the transits affect you personally, start with sign, then add the houses of your birth chart, then any natal planets being aspected. As you become more proficient, you will be able to do this intuitively, but to start with you will need to take each section at a time and overlay it onto the previous topic, making notes along the way.

Zodiac signs

We are all familiar with the twelve zodiac signs, but there is always more to learn. Here I discuss the qualities of each sign and how you can use them in transit astrology. Signs are grouped in order of appearance.

- Personal signs are concerned with the self and asserting the self, such as Aries.
- Interpersonal signs, such as Libra, are concerned with relationships and harmony.
- Transpersonal signs, such as Aquarius, are concerned with the group and society at large.

The colours, symbols, preoccupations and themes of each sign come into focus when the signs are viewed with an emphasis on the outer planets in that sign, as do pitfalls or shadow side. That is what we will be doing in this book: looking in particular at the transits. We tend to see the spectrum of possibilities expressed in a variety of ways. Be aware of what they are so you can recognize them and take the fastest route to astro power.

The constantly moving year

Since planets move through the zodiac in order, remember to note how the change occurs, building from one sign to the next. It may contrast one sign against another: new trends, fresh flavours and a new generation coming of age in the next sign that set themselves apart along its themes. When you're behind the times, it usually means you're still identifying with a sign of the times that's no longer relevant – usually the one from your heyday. As long as you love it, that's okay, just don't complain about the new vogue. Check the transits to understand the new vibe and you may begin to appreciate it!

♈

Aries

Mars · Red · Personal · Yang · Cardinal Fire

Aries is bold, active, energetic and pioneering. This is a sign of frontiers and, being first and a personal sign, is invested in the solo, individual, independent self. It's a me-first sign, a risk taker and ruled by Mars, so the assertive entrepreneur, warrior and athlete are all favoured. Explosions, fire, heat and even battles may be indicated as well as fitness, gyms and muscles!

Pitfalls · Issues may be around heat, fire, anger, violence, individual autonomy and independent action. On the positive side, it may be possible to address these issues.

Taurus

Venus · Earthy browns/greens · Personal · Yin · Fixed Earth

Taurus rules the Earth, the senses, values, nature. Farming, living off the land, and a return to nature may all come under its domain. Finance and money, housing and building are also under its auspices. Since it's a Venus-ruled sign, pleasure, comfort, practical arts and music may all feature when this sign is emphasized. Since Taurus is the personal Earth sign, it's concerned with the body, its care, nutrition and security. This is the slow food gourmet, so food may come into focus under Taurus skies.

Pitfalls · Issues around food security, the Earth and fertility, bodies, the senses and money.

Gemini

Mercury · Silver · Personal · Yang · Mutable Air

Gemini is personal Air so is concerned with the thought process, communication and vehicles of communication from reading, writing and learning, to even texting! It's a sign of intellectual curiosity, searching for data and facts rather than meaning, truth or high concepts. It moves from topic to topic quickly, gathers and disseminates information without judgement.

Pitfalls · Issues around clarity of communication, truth or manipulation of facts and data, lack of a clear narrative.

Cancer

Moon · Aquamarine · Personal · Yin · Cardinal Water

Cancer is a personal Water sign concerned with immediate connections, family, security and safety for the family. As a cardinal sign it seeks to connect emotionally and can be tribal looking after those it can. This sign is compassionate, non-judgemental and caring. Like Taurus this is a foody sign, but comfort and nostalgia are emphasized over the gourmet. Nurture, memories and traditional family values, or a focus on what constitutes family, may become areas of interest under Cancerian skies. This sign is subjective, so art and entertainment may reflect that quality. Expect soft flowing lines over hard stark contour.

Pitfalls · Issues around family, security, food, nurture or childhood, babies and parenting.

Leo

Sun · Yellow gold · Interpersonal · Yang · Fixed Fire

Leo is concerned with entertainment, the dramatic arts and luxury. The first of the interpersonal signs, Leo knows itself by interpreting its experience through drama and feedback from an audience. Expect a dance craze or renewed interest in dancing and arts as creative self-expression. The big personality, individual (as opposed to group), celebrity may be present under Leo skies. Leisure, leisure time and lifestyle are indicated.

Pitfalls · Issues with ego, cult of the personality, heart and circulatory system, and rampant individualism or narcissism.

♍ Virgo

Mercury · Lavender/white · Interpersonal · Yin · Mutable Earth

Virgo is a sign of service and economy. An Earth sign, it favours health, hygiene, nutrition and medicine. If times are tough under Virgo skies, this sign can get by and get things done on a tight budget. Professionalism and attention to detail is favoured with leaps in efficiency and proficiency expressed in some capacity. As a mutable sign ruled by quick-moving Mercury, planets in Virgo may indicate a time of movement and change. Jobs, work and the general daily workplace may come into focus. Humility and virtue are favoured.

Pitfalls · Lack of big-picture planning or awareness, too much fastidious focus on detail or economy.

♎ Libra

Venus · Pastels · Interpersonal · Yang · Cardinal Air

Since balance and harmony are vital to this sign, we may see issues of justice and equality arise. There may be a backlash to gains around equality, depending on the planets moving through Libra. Negotiation, mediation and compromise are preferred. Libra is ruled by Venus, so peace, beauty, aesthetics, love and relationships all feature. Expect the arts and entertainment and an emphasis on design.

Pitfalls · Binary gender roles, a focus on looks or aesthetics over substance, polite manners covering difficult truths or realities.

♏ Scorpio

Pluto · Red/black/purple · Interpersonal · Yin · Fixed Water

Scorpio rules the reproductive organs and is well known for delving into all things taboo. Secrets and manipulation may all be explored or exposed under Scorpio skies. Fashion can go dark, underground, a bit goth/emo. Scorpio is certainly ready to look at the more serious, psychological and metaphysical underpinnings of life. This sign is intense, puts sexuality on the table, and those difficult but all too human emotions around betrayal, love, jealousy, money and power. Scorpio's role is to detoxify and transform, so things could get dark before the dawn.

Pitfalls · Control may be a central issue. Scandals, abuse of power, people scapegoating the difficult issues, topics around sex and the resistance to facing or transforming society's guilt and shame.

Sagittarius

Jupiter · Orange · Transpersonal· Yang · Mutable Fire

The sign of optimism and expansion. Entertainment could be thought provoking, or it could give way to blockbuster experiences as this is a Fire sign that longs for stimulation and adventure. Comedy and humour are elevated. The seeker signifies international travel, exotic cultural exchange, spirituality and the occasional guru. Higher education, universities, colleges or modes of learning and philosophy may be featured. Prosperity may boom before it busts! Fashion and design may go over the top with exaggerated proportion. Borders, movement of people and immigration could feature along with independence, mobility and an active lifestyle. Animals, nature and the wilderness make a comeback.

Pitfalls · Overspending, economic bubbling, overconfidence, toxic positivity/no bad vibes, cultural appropriation and spiritual or philosophical dogma. International issues.

Capricorn

Saturn · Dark brown/navy/black · Transpersonal · Yin · Cardinal Earth

It's all about bossing up and business for this material Earth sign. Professional suits, looks and profiles with an emphasis on success, duty, tradition, status and responsibility are back in vogue. Capricorn may limit, focus and consolidate as well as represent structures, rules and restrictions. Governing bodies like the government, the boss, or people in authority are signified along with structure, systems and corporations. Following the sign of expansion, Capricorn is a sign of contraction, so this could be the bust after the boom. A realistic correction that is necessary but not fun at the time!

Pitfalls · Fear, depression, too much restriction or limitation, rules, loneliness or feeling isolated. Lack of love and emotional connections, walls or boundaries, burdens. Lack of personal authority. An economic pinch. Materialism or issues around economic structure.

Aquarius

Uranus · Electric blue/neon · Transpersonal · Yang · Fixed Air

This independent Air sign values science, rational and logical thought. Social activism, causes and human rights on the larger scale come into focus, while technology tends towards connecting the masses during this social sign's reign. A stripped back, glass, metal, spacious and airy, no-frills look dominates design while music may also reflect an electronic and airy, light, spacious sound.

Pitfalls · The individual sacrificed for the group. Group think. Over reliance on conceptual, rational thought and science. Too detached from everyday reality, nature or the body.

Pisces

Neptune · Soft pinks/metallics · Transpersonal · Yin · Mutable Water

When planets move through Pisces, fantasy, art and mystic themes are notable. Sensitivity and empathy are spotlighted. Fluidity or a blurring of boundaries, structures, rules, beliefs or perspectives may dissolve or open up. The iconic mythical or fantasy creatures like unicorns and mermaids may make an appearance, while new ways of escapism will be prevalent. Look to your dreams and symbols, while taking time to rest and go within. Being a Water sign, emphasis on mental and emotional health are highlighted, with a focus and acceptance of the more vulnerable in society.

Pitfalls · When the harsh realities of life present, escapism through addiction, drugs, fantasy or ditching responsibility are all fair game. Lack of boundaries, or a realistic appraisal, confusion, delusion, sensitivity to toxins, being duped. Issues with spirituality, sensitivity, creativity. Lack of energy.

Elements

There are four elements: Fire, Earth, Air and Water, which rotate in turn. Each element hosts three zodiac signs, which are four signs apart on the zodiac wheel and in your horoscope chart.

Fire

Aries · Leo · Sagittarius

Fire is energy, spirit and zealous, assertive action. It's yang and expressive. It can burn but it can also enliven and celebrate. It demands attention and is stimulating as well as excitable and exciting. It may literally denote heat, fire or something powered by a spark.

Earth

Taurus · Virgo · Capricorn

Earth is receptive, stabilizing and prefers the practical, useful, tangible building blocks, systems and routines in life. Earth eras bring focus to ecological issues, time, commerce, labour and production. These periods focus on the material side of life, things get built. Our bodies and natural environment come under the rulership of Earth.

Air

Gemini · Libra · Aquarius

Air is yang and seeks to connect through communication, learning and the social side of life. It suggests movement and the realm of ideas. It's cool, intellectual and can seem both impartial and impersonal. Air eras may express as leaps in communication – like the printing press or the internet. Things speed up in Air as it moves quickly without impediment with a focus on movement (of people) and connectivity generally.

Water

Cancer · Scorpio · Pisces

The Water element is yin or receptive, concerned with emotions, feelings and the subtle, psychic mode of non-linear or non-rational intelligence, like extra-sensory perception. Private and shy, the Water element points to our inner subjective experience. Water eras may result in awareness around our internal life, creativity, and they may reframe vulnerability. Sexuality and other areas that require merging and washing away strict boundaries, and even rules may come to the fore in these years.

Modes

There are three modes: cardinal, fixed and mutable.

Each mode (also known as a quality) hosts a sign from each element. That's four signs per mode. These are three signs apart at a square, a 45° angle to the last and next, thus each group forms a cross on the zodiac wheel: the cardinal cross, the fixed cross and the mutable cross. The mode or quality of a sign is not to be underestimated. Familiarize yourself with the basic meaning of the modes and how it fits into each sign along with the element.

Cardinal signs

Aries · Cancer · Libra · Capricorn
Cardinal is the go factor; they have a relentless quality of initiating in the element they are combined with and area the sign belongs to.

Fixed signs

Taurus · Leo · Scorpio · Aquarius
This is a hold-steady, don't-veer-from-course mode. Fixed signs have an enduring quality and like to stick to the plan. They don't change easily and prefer to stabilize, secure and fortify.

Mutable signs

Gemini · Virgo · Sagittarius · Pisces
Mutable is another way of saying change it up. Planets in mutable signs suggest a breaking down of structure, tweaking and adaptation. Multiple avenues of expression and versatility are common under mutable skies. Expect new perspectives and a challenge to consensus reality.

Aspects

From our position on the Earth, we map the stars as they orbit above us. At certain points, two or more planets will be at specific angles to each other, making what we call aspects.

Aspects are therefore a set of mathematical angles planets form to one another, connecting their functions. Some angles allow the energy to flow, representing ease; others show the planetary themes don't work together easily and will require effort and adjustment. Each aspect is determined by the distance between the planets involved. Depending on the planets and their aspect, different impacts will be felt in the astrological chart.

There are five major aspects. When planets are in these aspects to each other, then their qualities are modified by the influence of the other planet(s) – for better or worse, depending on the aspect.

- **Conjunction** – At 0°, this fuses and intensifies the two qualities, which is beneficial if they like each other, challenging if they don't.
- **Sextile** – At 60°, the planets will get on well as they stimulate each other.
- **Square** – At 90°, this is a tense aspect indicating conflict.
- **Trine** – This aspect, at 120°, releases the best qualities of both planets, as they work in harmony.
- **Opposition** – Polarity and competition to control are indicated here at 180°; compromise is needed.

Since each sign takes up exactly 30° of the full circle, it's easy to see, count or calculate certain aspects by looking at the degree of one planet compared to another. In a horoscope, they usually have aspect lines drawn from planet to planet. Depending on the program you use, they may provide a list for you. The little number next to a planet in a horoscope is the degree it is at in that sign. Each sign begins at 0° and ends at 29°.

Orb of influence

When transiting planets are forming an aspect to one or more natal planets or points in the chart, they exert their influence when they are precisely aspected and also for a few degrees either side. This is known as the orb of influence. A tight orb allows only a small angle when the planet is influential. It also makes a difference if the planets are moving towards the exact aspect (known as 'applying') or moving away (known as 'separating'). When transiting planets aspect your natal Sun and Moon, we usually use an orb of 10°. For other aspects, we might use a tighter orb of 5°.

The collective and the personal

On a collective level, an outer planet aspecting another outer planet is significant. You will feel part of the zeitgeist they represent if one or all are also aspecting a personal planet or point. Some people will use orbs of 10° or 15° as these slow processes catalyze events in society. You can see them coming and still processing way before an orb of 5° either way, so keep that in mind when comparing historical events to the astro weather at the time.

In a natal chart, the outer planets have more influence in an aspect than an inner planet, such as Pluto aspecting your Moon. In any aspect, you will see Pluto themes impacting lunar themes rather than the other way round. On a personal level, your emotional life (the Moon) will experience intensity (Pluto). A transiting outer planet aspecting a natal outer planet isn't going to be as significant unless there are natal inner planets mixed into the configuration.

Conjunction – merging

☌

0° together
Orb of 5° for the planets
Orb of 10° for the Sun or Moon

When planets are conjunct, they are together at the same degree of the same sign. You'll see them sitting together. Their themes are merged and must work together. Imagine a three-legged race – some work better than others! The outer planet will dominate and usually win, so the inner planet's themes need to work with it rather than resist. Conjunctions can go either way so they aren't good or bad, it depends on the planets involved and the set-up in your chart, as well as those themes in your life. Consider whether you're onboard with what they represent, resisting or ignoring this part of your life, or if you can accept the truths they represent. As with most things in life, the changing skies are a reminder that you really must be true to yourself.

This is the beginning of the synodic cycle between those planets.

When three or more planets are in orb of a conjunction (bunched together), this is called a stellium and amplifies themes of that sign and those planets. This area of your birth chart will be a focus over this period, so attend to it or plan ahead.

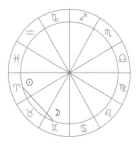

Sextile – stimulating

(asterisk symbol)

60° apart
Orb of 3° for the planets
Orb of 8° for the Sun and Moon

Similar to the trine aspect, the sextile offers opportunities as the signs hosting these planets are compatible, supportive and stimulating. They are Air/Fire or Earth/Water combinations and two signs apart. Take the opportunities and run with them or reach out and make things happen while the going is good.

Square – dynamic and challenging

(square symbol)

90° apart
Orb of 5° for the planets
Orb of 10° for the Sun and Moon

Squares hold the most dynamic tension. Built-up energy needs release. Squares represent themes that may clash as they are not easily integrated. Action is required! Check to see if it's an opening square (after the conjunction or before the opposition) or closing square (after the opposition).

They are three signs apart yet share the same mode, so a fixed square is stubborn and won't want to budge, a mutable square more easily adapts and melds, and a cardinal square may lock horns but push for some sort of way forward.

Collectively, a square between outer planets may express as two distinct sides or ideals that vie for power or dominance in a clash to release energy and drive change. It may be a critical or crisis point, but something has to give and generally does.

A faster-moving planet like the Moon or Mars entering the aspect configuration could trigger a release or expression in the form of an event.

In a natal chart, a transiting outer planet making a square aspect to a natal inner planet will feel very tense. You'll feel pressure to make a change and take action, so harness that energy and go with it. When resisted or ignored, it can result in inner tension, and perhaps an external event may happen seemingly out of your control, releasing the tension. It's better to take responsibility and make the change you need.

These periods can be extremely trying, but once the dust settles you'll be glad you took the bull by the horns! The issue can be hard to spot, identify with or accept because square aspects are like being blindsided. You can't see around the corner. The incoming archetype seems foreign, so it challenges your current world view or self-concept. Integrating it into your concept of how you see yourself may be part of the way forward. Outer planets are slow, so we get plenty of time to work it out, sometimes years.

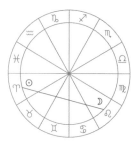

Trine – harmonious opportunity △

120° apart
Orb of 5° for the planets
Orb of 10° for the Sun and Moon

Planets that trine together, shine together. They are four signs apart and share the same element, speaking a similar language. Trines are the most beneficial and easy aspects. The planets work together in a flowing way, so you get the best of both, rather than the pitfalls. These periods of opportunity are worth planning for, knowing things will move well for you depending on which natal planet is picking up the flowing energy. Neptune in a trine with your Sun, for example, suggests extra sensitivity, empathy and artistry that you can express and identify with in a way that supports your sense of self (Sun). It suggests you easily identify with, benefit from and represent the zeitgeist or spirit of the times.

Consider how these energies could be harnessed when there is an outer planet in a trine aspect to one or more natal planets in your birth chart, or a trine between two or more transiting planets that are also forming a trine to a natal planet. Collect and enjoy the gifts rather than let them slip by.

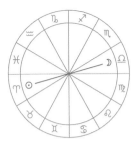

Opposition – a balancing act

180° opposite each other
Orb of 5° for the planets
Orb of 10° for the Sun and Moon

This is like the Full Moon phase of a synodic cycle, a fruition or peak, as well as a turning point and perhaps an opportunity to pivot.

Collectively, outer planets in opposition to each other have the most impact because they are so slow moving. Check back through the cycle to see what the themes may be and remember that the planets and signs involved will dictate what to expect.

When a transiting outer planet opposes an inner natal planet, you will likely identify with the inner personal planet while the outer planet may be projected. It could be experienced in the outer world as an event, situation or a person that fulfils the archetypal role, catalyzing emotions, a realization or situation. Oppositions can be easier to handle than the square because you're facing it and can see it. Once you can identify with and integrate themes of the transiting planet or make the change it suggests, this aspect may be easier.

Houses or temples

Every horoscope, whether it's your birth chart or a chart of an event, country or the current moment, has 12 segments. These are called houses or temples and they each represent a particular area of life. Planets transiting through these houses correlate with events in that area of life, so you know when it will begin and when it will end.

When a planet is transiting a house, it brings its themes to this area of life. Add the sign it is in for more information.

Get some detachment by leaning into your mythical imagination. See the house as a temple that planetary archetype is visiting. The word contemplate is related to the word temple and of course that was what the Ancients created these sacred spaces for. Contemplate on the archetypal nature and meaning of a transiting planet, and what it represents for you in the house it's in and the natal planet it is connecting with. Reflecting on the transiting planets in this way activates your symbolic mind, restoring the sacred to your life. It's a soulful way of approaching astrology and brings art to the science.

Houses, like signs, are in polarity to the house opposite them; they're on an axis. The beginning of each house is called a cusp. The 1st, 4th, 7th and 10th House cusps are particularly sensitive points, so planets forming a conjunction to them are significant.

Placidus house system

The modern house system uses the tropical zodiac and is called Placidus. The ascendant begins at the exact degree that was on the horizon the moment you were born. The signs are all 30° each, but houses may vary in size. In extreme northern and southern latitudes, the house system falls apart, so switch to whole-sign houses if that's the case. Traditional astrological knowledge has been translated over the last few decades through the hindsight project, so whole-sign houses have made a comeback. They begin at 0° of each sign. It's more generic but useful for techniques that were created for it. Indian Vedic astrology uses the sidereal zodiac, so be aware of the difference between these three variations if you're reading articles online and viewing clashing information.

Personal houses

1st House or ascendent · The 1st House begins with the ascendent. The sign on its cusp is called the rising sign. Lately it's been grouped in with the natal Sun and Moon signs as the third component of 'the big three' personal placements that are essential to your astrological interpretations. It rules the self, outlook, perspective, and how you approach new scenarios. This is the first of the Fire houses and in part describes your vital force, body and health. It's how you present and how people first perceive you when they meet you. Transits to the 1st House are powerful and could manifest as anything from changing your look to changing your direction. Crossing the ascendant from the 12th House, a planet becomes conscious, visible and impossible to ignore.

2nd House · This rules what belongs to you: money and income, your wealth and livelihood, your things, property and your values. This is known as the first of the Earth houses, so is material in nature. It represents your resources.

3rd House · This is the first of the social houses. It represents relationships based on proximity from your siblings to neighbours and your favourite barista downtown, the connections and exchanges of news as you go about your day. Short-distance travel within your own country is also represented by the 3rd House. It's on the communication and knowledge axis so rules early education, short courses, writing and learning. In traditional astrology, the interpretation of oracular information was included in this zone.

4th House · Also known as the IC or *imum coeli* (Latin for 'bottom of the sky') the 4th House represents your home, domestic scene, (chosen) family, family of origin and roots. As the first of the Water houses, it represents your emotional underpinnings and foundation. This zone may represent things hidden from view and is a private realm.

Interpersonal houses

5th House · This is concerned with creative self-expression, like your hobbies, what you do for fun, dating, sex, love affairs and romance. Children are signified in the 5th House since they are an act of creation. You'll find your inner child here, too. This is a house of creative expression, like a musical or artistic talent. It's the interest you do for pleasure, leisure and lifestyle that sparks joy. This zone also sees you enjoying the creative output of others.

6th House · The second Earth house rules work, work environment, colleagues and daily routines. Skills, service, duty and mentoring are signified here. As an Earth house, it's material so physical health and wellbeing are implicated, with the routines that underpin them, and the mind-body connection. This is where you go to self-care. Small pets or small animals appear here, since they anchor us in routine and support our wellbeing.

7th House · As the second Air house, also known as the DC or descendant, this is a social/relational house. Since the 1st House represents the self, it looks over at the other in the 7th. This house represents one-to-one equal relationships, including your partner, best friend or business partner. Planets passing through this zone may represent someone else who you experience its archetypal energy through, rather than directly. They may represent it or may be the one to experience the event signified by a transit here. Or you may experience it through the nature of the relationship itself. Contracts and agreements are signified, as are agents or those acting on behalf of another. Traditionally this is the house of open enemies, perhaps as love and hate are two sides of the same coin.

8th House · The second Water house, this zone signifies an interest in the occult, metaphysical and hidden side of life. Sex, death, psychology, intense experience, even crisis and transformation, as well as taxes and other people's money or resources are found here. Gains through others are indicated: inheritance, divorce or working with other's resources, like an investment banker. Everything taboo in your culture is swept into this zone. Like all Water houses, there's a sensitivity to the subtle, hidden and psychic level.

Transpersonal houses

9th House · The third of the Fire houses is on the communication, knowledge and travel axis, opposite the 3rd House. It rules experiences and vehicles that expand your mind, opportunities and your world in general. Higher education, philosophy, international travel, other cultures and teaching are found here. Large media, big corporations, educational and religious institutions are also part of this zone.

10th House · The 10th House is the top of your chart, so is known as the Midheaven or MC (*medium coeli*). It is the most visible, so it's all about reputation and how people see you from afar. It's the third of the material Earth houses and represents your career or vocation. It's time to boss up when planets hit this zone.

11th House · The third of the social houses, this one is all about groups, your friends, peers and people who share your ideals and interests. This is your tribe, your favourite social cause, whether you're socially active or into social activism. The socialite lives here, as do invitations and the desire to reach out and extend your circle. This is the ultimate girl-about-town placement. Your radar for trends and the larger social milieu is based here.

12th House · The final Water house, this is the zone of the mystic, ancestors and dreams. It's the place we go to transcend our everyday world, our concept of self and our ego. Your connection to the collective unconscious is through this zone. The other side of direct mystic experience is the urge to escape the reality of the mundane world, so find healthy ways to connect with spirit and the subtle energetic realms. Traditional astrology calls this the home of hidden enemies, perhaps they are the vices of escape! Don't let your ego trip you up. This zone doesn't tolerate selfishness; tune into the collective and have the best intentions beyond yourself. This zone requires solitude to get in touch with your subtle connection to the cosmos. Ashrams, spiritual retreats and even plant-medicine-assisted psychic journeys live here, as do mental health and channelling.

IV.

The planets

The luminaries

Sun · Moon

We refer to the Sun and Moon as planets in astrology, but they are more accurately called the luminaries or the lights; one to rule the day and one the night.

Most festivals are seasonal and the seasons occur because of the distance of the Earth from the Sun. Moonlight is simply reflected sunlight but it is equally important.

In astrology, the Sun and Moon are the most important of what we call the inner planets. They are sensitive points for interpreting transits, not as much for their transit of your chart but transits to your natal Sun and Moon. Although their cycle is one to watch, it's used a little differently from the outer planets. Modern science is still catching up with how they affect our body and moods.

Crossing irrelevant gender boundaries

Although gendered by many cultures through human history, they do gender swap in the cultural representation in various mythologies. It is a timely reminder not to project binary gender constructs onto them since their qualities belong equally to everyone.

The deity Ardhanarishivara, from Hindu religious mythology, embodies the concept of unity by being half lunar and half solar.

This reflects the fact that the qualities of the Sun and Moon are two halves of the same truth; one can't exist without the other – and neither can we, as the imbalance in our world demonstrates. This deity's message is that opposite qualities must embrace each other to generate and sustain our universe. Those qualities are the ideas we apply to the Moon and Sun, the passive and active forces, potential and kinetic energy, infinite and finite, yin and yang. In Ardhanarishivara's myth, the lesson is that you can't worship one and not the other equally.

Channels of energy

In Vedic teaching, these lunisolar qualities are represented as equal channels of energy that move up through the body; they're known as Ida and Pingala. The lunar channel represents the passive receptive, parasympathetic rest and digest mode. In contrast, the solar channel represents the active projecting channel. These cross at each chakra in the body, winding around the central channel, the Sushumna, in the spinal cord. They demonstrate that we need as much rest as we do activity. This system is represented in the West as the caduceus carried by Mercury, depicting two intertwined snakes.

Enlightenment is said to be via the middle path, balancing the duality of the solar and lunar channels, which are the sympathetic and parasympathetic nervous systems. There is no finding someone to be the Moon to your Sun or the Sun to your Moon; you must balance them in your body and your life to maintain wholeness.

Alternate nostril breathing

The two energy channels switch from right to left nostril dominance throughout the day and you can use a simple method of pranayama, or yoga breathing, to restore your system to balance and calm.

- Sit quietly and use your thumb to close your right nostril.
- Breathe in slowly and deeply through your left nostril.
- Release your thumb and close your left nostril with your ring finger.
- Breathe out slowly and fully through your right nostril.
- Breathe in through your right nostril, then out through your left.
- Do this five to ten times.

The Sun and Moon have long been timekeepers. While Western solar-focused society works off the Sun cycle, billions of people still use the Lunisolar calendar. Some cultures use both, with the lunar calendar marking religious events, holidays and festivals. For example, the Chinese New Year begins on the New Moon in Aquarius with celebrations over the waxing cycle and a grand finale two weeks later of the Full Moon in Leo. Luminous white balls that look suspiciously like the full orb of the Moon are exchanged, and lanterns are lit to celebrate light and growth as symbolized by the Moon at peak lunation.

Moon

☽ Moon

Sentire omnia · To feel everything (Cicero)
Keywords · Feeling centre · Emotional nature · Safety · Security ·
Nurture · Home · Family · Instinctual · Memory · Comfort food · Receptive ·
Changeable · Gut instincts · Mood · Belonging · Collective
Orbit · About 27.3 days, making 13 lunar months per year
In a sign · 2.3 days, passing through all 12 signs per lunar month
Rules · Cancer
Functions well · In Cancer and Taurus
Take special care · In Capricorn and Scorpio
Colours · Silver, luminous pearly white
Crystals · Moonstone, natural ocean pearl, opal
Metal · Silver
Function · Your emotional nature and what makes you feel secure and safe.
The language of care and nurture you give and respond to are lunar.

The Moon represents the night. When the light is turned down, we
lose the definition and colour of the day. However, the depths of
the universe, the stars in the sky and our inner life become apparent
in quiet tranquillity. It draws up instincts and feelings like the light
draws sea creatures to the surface of the ocean. The counterpart
to yang solar power, it's lunar yin, receptive and internal. The
Sun represents individual shine – how we separate and define
ourselves. The Moon is our awareness of interconnectedness,
commonality and community.

The limbic part of the brain is associated with what the Moon
represents: safety. When we go into our Moon placement to
explore our feelings and emotional needs, we may find ourselves
back in our inner child. Our brain stitches memory to feeling in
the limbic system, which is why the body can heal itself through
feelings. The body's somatic memory – which comes before words
– is a component of the mind and the body's intelligence, and a
type of consciousness. Somatic therapies are ideal for opening up,
unknotting and re-weaving emotional issues, especially trauma.

The Moon – the celestial body

One of two cosmic eyes, a lunar and solar, from our position on Earth, the Moon appears to be the same size as the Sun. It zips around our Earth much faster than any other heavenly body. Its rapid fluctuation represents the changeability of emotions. Feelings cycle naturally, they're not linear, and they're meant to flow like the Moon.

Because the transiting Moon moves quickly, don't pay it the attention the outer planets receive. However, because it is associated with mood and the emotional temperature day to day, it's handy to observe and plan by.

Being closest to Earth and orbiting us as we orbit the Sun, the Moon is about all things personal and represents the body's intelligence. It is cooling and calming, bringing moisture over its night-watch like the parasympathetic nervous system it's associated with. Slowing down is required for digestion, cleaning up cortisol after stress, and enjoying romance and intimate connection. Live by the Sun, love by the Moon!

The Moon – the deity

In Ancient times, life could be short, unpredictable and harsh. A deity could bring solace if you could turn to them for unconditional love, a listening ear and the power to answer your prayers. Both luminaries, as dependable as clockwork, were the perfect foil.

There are as many lunar deities as solar, with a variety of myths and gender representations. We're most familiar with the Great Mother Goddess as the nurturer. However, we've all heard of the man in the Moon; there's plenty of male lunar deities. Norse deity Mani is brother to Sol, his sister the Sun.

Like solar deities, the Moon is often depicted as being drawn across the sky by a charioteer (an Ancient favourite), in a basket or boat. Sometimes one luminary chased the other, were brother and sister, lovers, or referred to as the sacred marriage. Remember this means the perfect balance of lunar and solar, and can be gendered however you please, it's the qualities they represent that matter.

Ancient Greeks called the Moon Selene, Romans had Luna then Diana, who absorbed a variety of influences through the centuries. Thanks to the timekeeping role of the Moon, they became associated with birth and children among other things.

The Moon – the archetype

The Moon can represent a nurturing person and represents the inner primal needs for safety and security. This is the most tender, sensitive, private place within you. The lunar archetype is one of the feeder, carer, who enfolds you in their arms, listens to your feelings and prepares your favourite food! These days we're seeing more dads step into their nurturing side, address their feelings and express them. In fact, time spent with children engages the parental caregiving network in humans, regardless of gender.

We must take the gender expectation out of the lunar archetype to create an essential balance. Everybody feels, everyone has an emotional range, needs safety, security and love. The lunar scale is where we realize there's more strength in experiencing our feelings, expressing them or engaging a therapist to work through them.

The traditional view is outmoded and unhelpful. Women have been expected to do the emotional labour, then denigrated for having emotions. Men have been belittled for feeling or showing emotion and tenderness. The lunar archetype must be freed from being seen as feminine or a feminine trait. It implies and perpetuates the stereotype that females are naturally nurturing and emotional and defines lunar attributes as inherently feminine, excluding everyone else. It suggests masculinity is defined by not being emotional or nurturing. When you are working your Moon, you're inviting in the lunar archetype of the carer or nurturer, rather than working your 'feminine side'.

The Moon in transit on a collective level

The Moon signifies the changing mood of the collective according to zodiac sign, the quick aspects it makes, and the phase it's in.

Plan according to themes of each sign the Moon moves through. Aries is great for beginning something new, taking on a challenge or fitness. Leo is a fire sign associated with glamour, attention and creativity. Plan to see a show, hold a party or go for a show-stopping makeover.

The lunar cycle

The lunar cycle is the relationship between the Moon, the Sun and the Earth in a three-way dance of light and movement. As the Moon orbits the Earth and the Earth orbits the Sun, the changing alignment of the three bodies results in a cycle of the illuminated part of the Moon. Meanwhile, the Sun is moving through the zodiac signs. Knowing which zodiac sign the transiting Sun is in reveals which signs host the New and Full Moons. The New Moon is always in the same sign as the Sun. The Full Moon is always in the sign opposite the Sun's sign.

Manifesting with the Moon

The energy of each phase is different, so time your activities to suit the Moon's cycle. Since the Moon is connected to feelings and the body, feel your intentions as if they are manifest in the present; see yourself there now. This way, you're connected to your body and it's not just conceptual. Write out your intentions by hand, draw a vision board or create a ritual to help bring it to tangible reality. In the dark phase, you're planting seeds.

Waxing · When the Moon is waxing, do things you want to grow: like trim your hair, water your plants or begin something new. Over the waxing period, take steps to set your plans in motion. Follow the monthly cycle or plan for the intention to manifest six months later when the Full Moon is in the same sign.

Full · The Full Moon is all about high emotional energy, but it can be a little intense the days before it peaks. Once it hits that peak, it's in cruise mode, so keep that in mind. Getting out and being sociable or throwing a party is great around the Full Moon. Double down by choosing an extroverted sign that matches the atmosphere you're after, or a sign in line with the vibe you want. Scorpio Full Moons are sultry and intense, for example, when some people just want to be alone or in a small group.

When the Moon is full, ask that what you seek be revealed to you so that you become consciously aware of it. Revisit your list of intentions, journaling or vision board and call it in. This is harvest time; the fruit is ripe – pluck it!

Waning · When the Moon is waning, it correlates with slower growth, so trim what you don't want to grow, pull up weeds or wrap up a project.

The waning Moon is a time to enjoy your harvest, polish, perfect and consolidate your results. Wrap up as it darkens to the final crescent. Let go and let 'god/dess' as the cycle begins again.

New · From the dark to the New Moon is a quiet time of yin introspection. It's like the fertile ground of all being, so drop in, journal and ask yourself what it is you want.

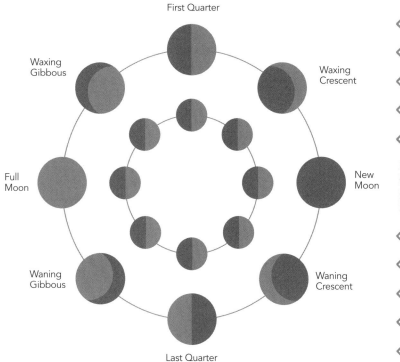

First Quarter

Waxing
Gibbous

Waxing
Crescent

Full
Moon

New
Moon

Waning
Gibbous

Waning
Crescent

Last Quarter

SUNLIGHT

The Moon in transit on a personal level

Outer planet transits to your natal Moon are major events, so look ahead and check dates. Easy aspects are something to look forward to, while challenging ones may rock your sense of emotional security, safety or connection. It may be time for more independence, to let go of someone, or to put up a boundary if your emotional connection is over or your needs aren't met or respected.

Food, home, family and digestion are all areas that could be implicated. Your awareness of what is going on – your litmus or canary in the cage – is your mood and feelings. If these are constantly in the red, stressed, anxious or depressed, it's time to do something about it. Listen, reflect, go within and self-care in ways that work for you. Check transits to your Moon for clues. As is often the case, painful triggers in the present often compound by catching something from the past. Reflect, like the Moon, by asking yourself when you have felt like this before. Your lunar side may offer up a memory, scenario or 'aha' moment if you give it the space.

Attachment theory speaks directly to your lunar side. It's worth understanding a basic framework to gauge your needs and responses.

If you need a method to open your mind to new possibilities, you might find the 'emotional freedom technique' of tapping is worth investigating. Based on the meridians and acupressure points, it is a simple hack to letting out the tears and pressure while getting to the heart of the issue. EFT involves repetitive tapping at specific points. Remember, though, that while it may relieve symptoms of pressure, you can't tap yourself out of a bad situation; you need boundaries or change in your environment.

The Moon transiting the houses of your birth chart

When the Moon transits through your birth chart, the house becomes the temple of the Moon. If you know the Moon's sign in your birth chart, follow the lunar cycle and note how you feel each time the Moon is back in that same sign. What about when it crosses your ascendant or your midheaven? You can plan by sign, and you can plan by the house the Moon is going to be in at any particular time. If the Moon is in a specific house, look at it as the temple of the Moon. What do you need to offer to the Moon in this temple? Suppose it's your 10th House of career and public image. In that case, you may feel like connecting and sharing publicly by going out or showing up online and doing a live chat. On your ascendant, you may feel more vulnerable yet still able to connect with people.

Pay close attention to the Moon's orbit in relation to the sign and its placement through your birth chart and take notes. That way, you can plan with the knowledge that yes, you do feel like connecting when the Moon is in your career zone or no, it's about the grind. You may feel like working behind the scenes on a longer-term project.

The Moon transiting the natal planets of your birth chart

When a planet is transiting your natal Moon, you can work your Moon. You have two lights, solar and lunar, that are cosmic eyes – use them both! Working your Moon means feeling your emotional life with acceptance, listen to your gut instincts. They pick up on everything and are a super-power; place that lunar jewel in your crown.

Moon in a sign

Our bodies are sensitive to the changing light of the Sun and Moon, possibly the magnetic charge of the tides, and so many other intricacies science has yet to discover. Everyone generally feels more energized and outgoing at the Full Moon and internal over the dark Moon. People who have a menstrual cycle are often well aware of the Moon's monthly orbit in connection with their body, energy and emotional cycle. Ovulation is associated with the Full

Moon as the light is bright; fertility is at its peak and the hormonal balance is geared towards extroversion. As the light empties, hormones dump, moods dump and the body dumps. This is the best time to be alone and let go of the last month. As feelings are amplified, notice what your body is bringing to your awareness in those impossible-to-ignore red flags. On the next waxing cycle, it's time to deal, make changes and take the next evolution towards a project or goal. Track the cycle and see how you feel as the Moon changes sign, waxes and wanes.

Getting back in tune with the Moon

Since we have so much artificial light, we have less chance to sync with the Moon, which means we're not in sync collectively. To sync your internal rhythms, try this.

- Keep a light on over the Full Moon or a curtain or blind open if it's bright outside.
- Over the rest of the month, keep your room completely dark while you sleep.
- Use twilight lights that automatically warm to amber as the Sun sets, ambient lighting, and blue-blocker glasses if you're on a screen after sunset.
- Be sure to get plenty of morning sunlight to help reset.

Work your Moon

Self-care lunar style means paying attention to your emotional needs, developing your sensitive side, and listening to that part of yourself with curiosity and non-judgement. The reward is a rich emotional connection with yourself and your intuition, as well as with others. A happy Moon is a healthy Moon.

EQ, emotional intelligence, ranks higher than IQ when it comes to success. No one is essentially self-made; we are group animals and thrive through warmth and connectivity, like all mammals.

Moon milestones – lunar returns

Every 27.3 days, as the Moon passes over the exact degree of the sign it is placed in your birth chart, you experience a lunar return. Calculate a chart for this moment to gauge the emotional tone of the month ahead. Look at the rising sign for flavour, and aspects to the Moon. Or keep it simple and create a mini ritual to celebrate and set intentions for the next cycle. It's a great way to honour your inner life and feelings. Include a monthly dialogue with your body by asking questions and waiting for a response through feeling, an image, sensation or memory. Each sign has a different way of expressing and responding to their lunar return. Natal Scorpio Moons may want privacy to attend to their secrets, while natal Libra Moons may prefer to chat or hang out in an art space, Champagne in hand, adding to their collection. There's no one size fits all.

Personal challenges and pitfalls of the Moon

Your feelings are valid, but don't let them define you. Remember, they're changeable. The Moon is associated with the Water element so, like water, feelings must flow. Blocking or repressing your feelings means the energy must go somewhere else. Repressed feelings will depress and build as depression, then burst through as anger, rage or violence. Listen to what they're telling you and work from where you are rather than be ashamed. Own your feelings for self-care, wellbeing and healthy loving connections. Anger is okay; it's righteous and telling you something is over the line, or you don't feel safe or secure. Respect it and respond. Anger fuels action; let it power you to correct what has become imbalanced, set a clear boundary, speak up or push something out of your space. Take time to figure out what has made you angry, sad or irritable before responding. Your reaction should be appropriate and properly directed.

The lunar consciousness is as essential to wholeness as night is to day. However, solar consciousness has been raised and privileged while lunar has been demoted. For wellbeing and wholeness, we need to embrace and tap into both types of consciousness.

The Moon out of bounds

The Moon slips out of bounds regularly every month over a ten-year stint, alternating with ten years staying within the bounds of the Sun. 2020 right through 2029 is an out-of-bounds Moon cycle. Since planets head beyond the boundary of the Sun when in Gemini/Cancer and Sagittarius/Capricorn, these signs add their flavour to the influence. The area of your birth chart ruled by these signs is where the Moon may be OOB, while other areas will never play host to this renegade emotional vent.

To understand how this transit shows up in your life, track the OOB Moons and keep a log. If you have a natal OOB Moon, the influence may exaggerate your already unfettered emotional nature and you may feel more free, liberated and able to make change if you've been complying with expectations instead of what you know is right for you. For the rest of us, we might get some necessary detachment, space, openness or emancipation. A general rule of thumb with planets OOB is to run your spontaneous plan by your sensible friend, or sleep on it if it's a drastic emotional change, quite out of the ordinary, a risk or over-share. Tap into the collective, popular culture or transcend it to come up with an intuitive, out-of-the-box spark of genius. Note the pings of your gut intel.

Try a sharing circle where everyone speaks on a topic; it's revealing, especially with a group of strangers. There's an Ancient quality to it, and the bonding is entirely lunar. It is best done around a flame under the moonlight or set up a circle with your friends and pass the talking stick, each one taking their turn without interruption as they hold the stick.

Astro Power

Sun

Sun

Sol invictus · The unconquered Sun

Keywords · Vital force · Central organizing principle · Conscious awareness · Charisma · Personality · Will power · Visibility · Self-expression · Self-esteem · Ego · Self-actualization · Courage · Sovereign · Magnificent

Orbit · One year

In a sign · 30 days

Rules · Leo

Functions well · In Leo and Aries

Take special care · In Aquarius and Libra

Colours · Gold, yellows, oranges and reds

Crystals · Diamond, amber, ruby, yellow topaz

Metal · Gold

Function · The solar principle represents the light of consciousness and awareness. It's yang, and its function is to give life, express and be seen. In astrology it represents the ego, self and identity. When you say I, me, mine, or I am, you're speaking from the part of yourself represented by the Sun. It's how you shine and express yourself in the world. Confidence and self-esteem are vital to shine and contribute, creating a feedback loop that enhances our life force with positive attention. The Sun is how we impact our environment and make an impression, like a dialled-up Leo living their best life.

The Sun – the celestial body

The heart and engine of our solar system, the Sun is our central organizing principle thanks to its gravitational pull. It is self-powered through ongoing nuclear fusion, as proton atoms collide within its core, creating helium atoms producing its own heat, light and radiation. Technically, this means the Sun is the only true star in our solar system, while planets twinkle, reflecting its light.

The Sun – the deity

The Sun is represented by a rich and vast array of deities, since every culture creates myths around our solar source of life. Overlaid with spiritual significance as an embodiment or extension of the supreme deity, its stories of goddesses and gods range from the cosmic eye to many a chariot towing the Sun across the sky each day. The personifications were assigned gender so we could see ourselves reflected in them, the Sun being traditionally male in Ancient Greece and Rome. In earlier times, however, the supreme deity was assigned a female gender since the great creator gave birth to all that exists. She was called the Goddess with a thousand faces, meaning everything was an emanation of her, that everything has an element of divinity. As we now know, everything is indeed moving energy and mostly composed of space.

Myths represent the culture that creates them as well as instructing the next generation. As patriarchal cultures clashed with matriarchal, they rewrote the myths over time to reflect their values, swapping out women for men as the central organizing principle of society, law and family.

The solar story and that of the supreme creator is essentially the most important since it is used to establish the divine right of whoever it resembles. Many male historians and archaeologists have tended to view history through their own lens, dismissing anything not fitting an androcentric narrative or gendering it male. But there are plenty of others to investigate. Celtic solar deities were female and, of course, the Norse/Germanic Sun goddess Sunne/Sowilo/Sol is where we derive our current word Sun. There are many more to choose from. The rising Sun on the Japanese flag is the emblem of the Shinto Sun goddess Amaterasu. The American Cherokees' Unelanuhi means proportioner of time. Or get creative like the Sun and intuit your own version.

Having a deity for everything from doorways to the dawn, the populated pantheon of Greco-Rome featured many aspects of light and the day, including Helios, Apollo and Eos. Looking for a power couple? There's also duel solar deities for a binary but equal representation.

The Sun – the archetype

Mythologizing of the Sun comes in a vast array of stories and the archetype is the core meaning that each of us must find and channel in a human and tangible way. This is why it's essential we choose a model that supports us to live our best life, confidently embracing our destiny. The Sun shines without end and represents your birthright to shine too.

Like the celestial Sun, the archetype of the Sun is embodied by anyone who is a central figure: monarch, leader, VIP, celebrity or star. This is the BIG personality that is warm, fills and commands a room, if not a stadium. It represents confident, healthy self-esteem. Putting the soul back into sol, it's your destiny to remove the blinders and emit your light, talent and soul purpose.

Is the lion the king of the jungle? In fact, she's the queen! The lion has long been a symbol of the Sun and the sign it rules, Leo. Early images portray a lioness with a female deity and in the wild it's the females that are together for life, while the males move from pride to pride. The females are egalitarian, sharing food and raising cubs communally. They work together to do most of the hunting, can protect their turf and cubs, as well as expand their territory. Lion social structure flies in the face of the usual reading of the Sun, both of which have been misused to reinforce hyper-masculine, patriarchal stereotypes when it is an excellent reminder of other ways to structure society and shine brighter together.

The Sun in transit on a collective level

The movements of the planets have an effect both on the general zeitgeist and on individuals.

The Sun in a sign -- the solar cross and wheel of the seasons

While not as impactful when forecasting, the Sun creates our day and night and seasons as we spin and orbit around it. Many cultures have symbolized the Sun's orbit as a circle enclosing a cross. This cross represents the four points at which the seasons change, marking the solstice and equinox points. They begin at 0° of each cardinal sign, which are Aries (spring equinox), Cancer (summer solstice), Libra (autumn equinox), Capricorn (winter equinox) and the opposite seasons, but same signs, in the southern hemisphere. Festivals at these times are solar celebrations for the agricultural season – they are festivals of light.

Anthropomorphizing the Sun's return

At the winter solstice, the Sun appears to stand still for three days at its weakest and lowest point in the sky. This was written into mytho-poetic stories by northern cultures that depend on summer's return for survival. The story represents the death or dying of the Sun, then its rebirth as it begins to rise again from this point, bringing longer, warmer days. This is the Christian holiday of Christmas on 25 December as the Sun reappears. The Sun is seen as representing the birth of Christ as an emanation of the supreme creative power of the universe. Tangible and based on survival, the holiness of nature's cycle, and the return of the saviour, the Sun!

The Sun in transit on a personal level

While transits of the Sun are quick in tempo, it's the transits of the outer planets to your natal Sun that count. To keep our inner combustion engine firing, we need the right environment to thrive. Keep a close eye on what's coming up to aspect your Sun and when. These mark the cosmic clock chiming a challenge or opportunity to your sense of self, identity, self-awareness, self-expression and growth. Take up the challenge as though your life depends on it and treat your life and those of others with reverence. This is your divinity and theirs, since life is sacred.

The Sun transiting the natal houses of your birth chart

The Sun lights up the affairs of the house it's transiting through, bringing attention, activity and awareness. Use the focus to spotlight that area of your life through the year.

Note when the solar chariot will be passing over points like the top of your chart and your ascendant. You can expect these to be times when you get noticed. Winning a prize or award is a classic manifestation. Utilize the transit by planning ahead, knowing which area of life the Sun will be lighting up, and when.

The Sun may represent a person in charge, or perhaps it's your chance to step up and pitch, vie for a raise or share what you're doing by launching a project.

The Sun transiting the natal planets of your birth chart

When the Sun aspects planets in your natal chart, while not a big impact, it will light them up and draw attention to them. Watch the solar cycle in relation to your natal Sun.

- When the Sun is in a sign of the same element as your Sun, it forms a trine, suggesting your ability to express yourself is in harmony with that time of year.
- The sextile will be in signs that are compatible with your Sun sign, suggesting these seasons support the way you express your solar self. In a flowing aspect to your Venus, your desires and the way you relate are supported.
- Conjunct your north node? See what lights up over those days; it could be a clue to your destiny or a step you don't want to miss.

Work your solar power

Make an entrance and an impression. Blast your solar power! Here's how. Check the degree of your natal Sun. Each day, that degree of your zodiac Sun sign will rise over the horizon. Use a transits chart to progress forward and backward in time to see when your zodiac sign will be rising for a specific day/event/meeting. Each sign takes two hours to rise. Another way to explain it is that your sign is on the transiting chart's ascendant as the rising sign for two hours each day. If you have a meeting or moment, arrange it for the time when your sign is rising. Experiment – you get a chance to test this daily.

Sun milestones – solar returns

The Sun's return to the exact degree and minute you were born is called the solar return – aka your birthday. No wonder you're the centre of attention, honoured with gifts and made a fuss of – it's all on-brand for this solar celebration. The Sun is personal, so it's meant to be all about you. The exact return may fall on the day before, the day or the day after the date you were actually born. Like setting intentions on New Moons, set a solar intention once a year on this part of the cycle as it's the beginning of your personal annual solar cycle. Set intentions around your identity, expansion, enlightenment and vitality, what you want to shine into the world and how you wish to be seen. Visualize and feel it as already existing. Make a wish as you blow out your birthday candles.

Personal challenges and pitfalls of the Sun

The transiting Sun doesn't pose serious pitfalls, although it could move into an already tense aspect configuration and trigger it.

Coverture and identity

Too much or too little can be the issue with the Sun. The gender bias can be a pitfall here, as historically the Sun has shone on the male half of society at the expense of the female, expecting that to dim it down, take up less space and support the others' Sun at the price of its own. The same can be said for ethnic minorities and anyone not fitting into society's favoured yet arbitrary divisions. There is no reason why you should give in to the outdated notions of coverture – giving up your identity to your husband.

Your name is how you are identified and the expectation that a woman takes her husband's name is symbolic of the patriarchal practice that saw women as property, owned by their father, husband or son. The march of history tended to exacerbate this imbalance and only now are we beginning to fight back and reclaim our half of the limelight.

This means that you may have a journey to reclaim your full solar power because you are having to deal with so many pressures from the past, such a weight of expectation. However, knowing why our society is so laden with pitfalls – from language to law – helps us to avoid them and not take them personally, as well as the confidence to call them out. Astrology reminds us we all have a Sun of equal value. We were born to shine equally, even if society hasn't caught up! If a narrative or situation seems unfair or unequal, always 'flip it and reverse it', as Missy Elliot sang.

The god complex

The ego and identity – our rational, conscious side – are essential, but they must be balanced by the spiritual, emotional and symbolic, like the solar day is balanced by the lunar night.

If the Sun is allowed to become totally dominant – think of the divine right of kings, monarchs believing themselves to be an embodiment of a deity, or political dictators – the Sun is imbalanced. This is known as a 'god complex'. At the other end of the scale, when there's not enough solar strength, we lose touch completely with our sense of self. If we are all 'day', the Sun will burn us up; if we are all 'night', we'll be left feeling low and unenergized. Transits by the Sun aren't potent, but transits to the natal Sun are. They call for evolution, tread consciously on your path towards your unfoldment.

Icarus

The story of Icarus – the boy given wings to escape imprisonment but who arrogantly flew too close to the Sun, which melted the wax on his wings – reminds us of moderation and sticking to our goals rather than being caught in the short-lived but heady winds of ego, losing sight of our flight path towards our destiny. It also suggests the truth of our being is so bright that it could melt our identity too fast. There's a reason a firewall exists between our conscious (solar) and subconscious (lunar) awareness. Enlightenment or illumination is a journey as well as a destination.

Transits to our Sun bring these gifts and challenges onto life's stage, highlighting them. They're opportunities to recognize, re-organize and make decisions that put you in a position of strength and vitality. Choose your destiny wisely.

The inner or personal planets

Mercury · Venus · Mars

These planets move quickly, so don't have the grinding impact of the outer planets. They show up personally in ever-changing energy and style, dancing through your chart as mood, lighting, meetings and inspirations.

Mercury

☿ Mercury

Cogito ergo sum · I think therefore I am (René Descartes)

Keywords · Thought · Mind · Communication · Messages · Information · Perception · Speech · Listening · Writing · Connections · Neural synapses · Cognitive process · Critical thought · Interpreter · Guide · Herald · Deliveries · Exchange · Information and its pathway

Orbit · 11–13 months

In a sign · 15–67 days

Rules · Gemini and Virgo

Functions well · In Gemini and Virgo

Take special care · In Sagittarius and Pisces

Colours · Silver; the fresh, cooling and calming colours of nature

Crystals · Diamond, emerald, peridot

Metal · Quicksilver

Function · Mercury is the messenger of the zodiac; its functions are critical analysis, communication and exchange. It connects thoughts and concepts, sharing them through speech, writing and visual communication. It rules everything associated with information and delivery, from the postal van to your digital device, from point A to point Z.

Mercury – the planet

Positioned between the Sun and the Earth, Mercury is seen as the interpreter and messenger – whether you believe that is of the gods, the soul or the Sun. Together with the Moon, Mercury has the quickest orbit, and both are associated with aspects of the mind and memory.

Mercury – the deity

The Ancient Greek version of the messenger was Hermes, renamed Mercury by the Romans. These deities also have qualities of earlier deities from goddess cultures combined into their meaning and therefore have many jobs to fill. As the messenger of the god/dess, Mercury is the only deity with an all-access pass not just to the Earth but to the heavens and the underworld. Just like the metal, Mercury is always on the move.

Transformation and healing are recurrent themes, and this may speak to Mercury's rulership of Virgo. In myth, Mercury functions as a guide, delivering souls as well as messages. The expression 'don't shoot the messenger' derived from the fact that they used to do exactly that if a messenger brought bad news – but it helped to preserve the mercurial aspect. Mercury holds a caduceus, originally an olive branch or staff signalling their neutrality. The symbolism of the winding snakes brings the DNA helix to the modern mind – the cells that hold the knowledge of life – but certainly the duality yet balance represented by the twin snakes has always designated compromise and communication. The symbol is supposed to have originated when Mercury threw his staff at two snakes to stop them fighting. It also suggests the kundalini pathway, meeting at the top in the liberation of consciousness.

Mercury is depicted as youthful because curiosity, agility and a nimble mind are essential at every age. Ever spritely, the winged sandals and hat represent speed and being always on the go – like our minds.

Moving between day and night, Mercury is associated with duality and contrast, such as the communication between the two sides of our brain. When we give precedence to the rational left brain over the creative and symbolic right brain, we move out of balance and invite mental health issues. As the Sun and Moon are complementary and necessary opposites, Mercury connects these two modes of consciousness.

In astrology, Mercury takes on the qualities of the planet it aspects. In myth, Hermes is often teamed up with other deities and was sometimes represented in Hermae pillars with a head carved on the top, some featuring Hermes combined with another deity. Teamed with Aphrodite to form Hermaphoditos, we can perhaps interpret as an erotic deity with a spectacular bedside manner!

Related to Hermes, the double-headed deity, Janus, looked back on the road they'd travelled and ahead into the future, another reference to perspective and the multiplicitous nature of the mind.

Visible fleetingly at the threshold of twilight, Mercury is associated with thresholds, doorways and crossings, the point of connection. Both guiders of souls, as a psychopomp, Mercury leads Sol over the twilight threshold into the underworld of night, then, as a psychagogos, escorts the Sun/soul/solar consciousness back through the in-between time of night into day. The same could be said for transitioning through various stages of wakefulness and sleep. The trick of remaining or regaining consciousness once asleep is called lucid dreaming and is truly Mercury in night mode.

Mercury – the archetype

The blogger, analyst, reporter, witty raconteur, wordsmith, side hustler and midnight rustler have archetypal Mercurial and mercantile components.

Greek Hermes reveals the trickster component of this archetype. The clever and cunning mind, solving problems or creating them! However, the mind can also play tricks on you; it's a fabulous servant but a terrible master. Give Mercury unfettered freedom, but don't let it think it owns the road.

Most, if not all, cultures feature a trickster archetype. In Native American cultures, Wiley Coyote often embodied this aspect of Mercury. There's a lot of shapeshifting, gender-bending and mistaken identity, which makes for excellent comedic and dramatic material. You'll see the trickster archetype show up repeatedly in literature, film and culture. Loki, the Norse deity, has found a contemporary audience via the Thor series. Also not playing by the rules is Viola in Shakespeare's Twelfth Night, Captain Jack

Sparrow and the prankster Weasley twins in the Harry Potter series. Tricksters break out of binaries, often possess magic and open the mind to possibility. They use humour, ruse and wit, invert consensus reality and rules, may be affable or villainous, but are most likely a paradox. English comedian turned socio-political commentator Russell Brand is a poster child for this archetype; a Mercury-ruled Gemini.

Mercury in transit on a collective level

Mercury is never more than 28° away from the Sun, so it will only ever be in the preceding, the same or the proceeding sign. The nature of the sign suggests the style and quality of communication and interest. It may be unclear if you want directions but great for artistic pursuits during Pisces, assertive and fresh during Aries or chatty during Gemini. Aspecting another planet, comms may be sharp, direct or argumentative if it's Mars, pleasurable but not direct when it's Venus – unless Venus is in Aries, enhancing assertiveness with a smile.

Mercury in transit on a personal level

Mercury's transits are fast, so it's not essential to look out for unless the retrograde aspects major natal planets or points. Of more importance are outer planet transits to your natal Mercury. In this case, it may be writer's block, cosmic download or mind blown. You may feel a lack of clarity or ability to express yourself coherently while Neptune aspects. Poetry or songwriting talent may be born, or at least a new appreciation develops.

Mercury transiting the house of your birth chart

Mercury's quick transits may deliver a message in this area of life, show up as a Mercurial type or perhaps it's you who needs to communicate here. Consider what this deity wants from you in this area of life: to deliver, or for you to deliver? Keep an eye out for the many guises the messenger or the trickster may take. Things may speed up in this area of life; you might be busy moving about, taking short trips or humming with great ideas. Take the time to chat with people associated with the area; they may have a message for you! Use your intuition; are you drawn to someone in particular? Do they stand out positively? Go say hi and see why.

Mercury transiting the natal planets of your birth chart

As Mercury aspects various natal planets, this may externalize as an event, connecting the houses involved. Perhaps you have intel, a realization or ability to express that planet. Conjunct the Sun and you're talkative, able to express yourself or connect with your soul clearly on a matter. Conjunct Venus, and you're being chatted up, or is that you making the advances? Conjunct Mars, and you may act on your ideas or have guidance on how to act.

Mercury makes an annual return, so keep the date handy and observe. This is the beginning of a new cycle, so set your intentions on what you want to achieve intellectually or in areas ruled by Mercury, especially according to the sign your natal Mercury is in. The spiritual expression of Mercury is an awareness of the mind, the duality of looking into a mirror and seeing oneself, the true nature of reality. This is a good time for meditation and contemplation.

Work your Mercury

Respect your mercurial faculties, don't wait to be asked, and question narratives that don't have your best interests at heart. Gather a variety of intel and be confident in your ideas, thought processes and ability to communicate them. Feed and cultivate your mind, and pursue your interests because, like Mercury, life is fleeting; develop and seed the world with your unique brilliance. If someone calls a gender, ethnic, age or any other card, speak up louder. Your voice matters.

Personal challenges and pitfalls of Mercury

Since Mercury is always on the go and rules the nervous system, be sure to get plenty of rest if you feel you're too up in your head. Ground into your body. Watch for the transits that may leave you feeling mentally fatigued or gullible (like Neptune) and utilize them for what they're designed to do. Honour each sacred point the cosmic clock chimes. For example, learn and expand your mind when Jupiter transits your natal Mercury; be willing to experiment and consider new ideas and concepts when Uranus transits.

Mercury retrograde

Retrogrades last for about three weeks, three times a year and move 8–15° each time.

Mercury retrogrades move through the elements. The degree Mercury turns retrograde is the degree it turned direct three cycles previous, eleven months prior. It goes back, picks up, relinks and weaves the thread back in, or at least this is your opportunity to do so.

Messages may come in the form of dreams, synchronicity while watching a film, or lyrics that suddenly amplify as your mind connects to a particular topic. Perhaps someone returns, you find yourself remembering a specific scenario from years ago; they're the fleet-footed messenger dashing by. It's up to you to catch and interpret while trusting your ability to do so.

Our culture is increasingly Mercurial, data and digital device-driven. When Mercury retrogrades, it snatches headlines encouraging panic. One of astrology's most well-known happenings, besides birthdays, lunar phases and the Saturn return, must be Mercury's thrice-a-year backspin that sends our best-laid plans into freefall, or at least give us pause to reflect, reconsider and redo. Tweaking and course correction are valuable ways to make the most of this period. Many problems can be created by undue haste, cutting corners and being ill-prepared.

Mercury conjuncts the Sun twice during the retrograde cycle, filling with Solar consciousness. What expresses or becomes clear over this period? Keep a journal over the Mercury retrograde cycle, including the pre-retro-shade and post-retro-shade, and it may reveal invaluable clues. The continuity and cohesion will enable insight and reflection to connect to the symbolic and lunar side of your consciousness, restoring balance. This is the process of remembering. Rather than barrelling along at top speed without reflection and space to learn from your journey, you can plan ahead.

The general rule of thumb is to time significant travel, events, launches or contracts so Mercury is moving direct and not retrograde if you can help it. More information coming to light over the retrograde may be worth waiting for. Triple-check everything and take things more slowly and thoroughly than usual or you're likely to trip up on an overlooked detail, like sending a text about someone to them.

Mercury out of bounds

Mercury is OOB 13% of the time, so watch for these periods as they're great for thinking outside the box. You might catch wind of intel you normally wouldn't. Watch popular culture to see if anyone lets the cat out of the bag, gaffs or speaks out of character. When Mercury is OOB, be mindful that this may not be the time to send that email to your boss saying what you really think.

Venus

♀ Venus

Amor vincent omnia · Love conquers all (Virgil)

Keywords · Love · Pleasure · Relational · Harmony · Values · Aesthetics · Arts · Beauty · Design · Charm · Desire · Attraction · Refinement · Luxury · Civilizing · Wealth · Affection

Orbit · 10–14 months, averaging 1 year

In a sign · 25–125 days when Rx, averaging 1 month

Rules · Taurus, Libra

Functions well · In Taurus, Libra and Pisces

Take special care · In Aries, Virgo and Scorpio

Colours · Pastels, soft floral colours

Crystals · Diamond, white sapphire

Metal · Copper

Function · Discerning and receptive, Venus governs relationships, the principle of love, desire, attraction and style. It's how we receive and share affection, express what pleases us and create pleasure in our lives. Pleasure through love, beauty, the arts, sensuality all involves a certain harmony of symmetry, which is at the basis of what we find attractive. Venus and Mars intertwine as aspects of sexuality. What and who you find attractive turns you on; desire and eroticism are all Venus. Venus refines and civilizes. It creates an awareness of others, negotiating an outcome that works for more than the individual.

Mercury is the exchange, Venus is the value of the exchange, so it's also associated with money and wealth. It's your relationship to wealth and resources; how you value yourself may indicate what you know you deserve! While Mercury rules dexterity and might dominate among people and trades like weaving or sales, the ability to create and express beauty is Venusian, so arts and crafts are under its rulership.

Venus – the planet

Anything but cool, this planet of passion runs a sultry 482°C (899°F), coming in as the hottest planet in our solar system besides the Sun; it's a sobering premonition of what will happen if we don't do what this planet represents and all get along.

Affiliated with the metal copper because it's attractive, malleable, gathers heat and conducts, the role of Venus is also the gatherer and conductor of the group, of collections and social aspects.

From our point of view on Earth, Venus is never more than 48° away from the Sun. It's easy to find with a maximum of just over one and a half signs ahead or behind.

Venus is only visible as the evening and morning star. The evening version is ahead of the Sun and said to be the lover, wise and reflective. From this point, it begins a retrograde every 19 months, appearing to 'fall' or drop from a high point until disappearing as it passes the setting Sun. From this point, the star is invisible until reappearing in the early hours as the morning star.

Its cycle is the most symmetrical and its retrograde cycle creates a five-pointed star or pentagram. An entire cycle takes eight years to complete. Continue tracing out the cycle to see a beautiful five-petalled rose pattern form; no wonder this planet is associated with beauty and harmony. Like a cosmic diamond, it sparkles brightest against the inky firmament. Reflecting 70% of the Sun's light, only 3% reaches its surface, creating ambient light for the deity of love.

Venus – the deity

Mighty Aphrodite for the Greeks, Venus for the Romans, the goddess of love, beauty and desire is said to have birthed from the sea foam (aphros means foam) near Cyprus after Saturn castrated his father, Uranus, and threw his genitals into the sea. Like so many tales, a seed of historical truth is woven into myth. Venus was indeed from Cyprus, where she slowly morphed into what we are more familiar with today. At that time, she held primacy as a sexually potent fertility deity.

The Lady of Lemba is a 5,000-year-old artefact with pronounced sexuality, merging a female body and vulva with a phallic head. Eventually, absorbing Inanna/Ishtar, armed and fierce, from the Near/Middle East, this deity struck fear and terror in hearts and minds. She was the protector, called on for life through fertility, while death was her whim. This incarnation was woman, bird and beast rolled into one.

The Greeks landed in Cyprus around 1200BC. Impressed with the lady of Cyprus, they took her mainstream, Aegean style, as Aphrodite. Her main sanctuary was established in Paphos.

Everyone, particularly women, worshipped her. Tended by priestesses, she occasionally gender-swapped as the bearded Aphrodite artefact reveals. The point being she supported the spectrum and surge of sexuality. Along the way, she laid down her arms. Making love, not war, her qualities became focused on beauty, love, desire, tenderness, and their variety of expressions.

Ancient Greeks had a deity to embody everything in the passionate spectrum, from Aphrodite Harmonia (union) through to Aphrodite Melania (Aphrodite of the dark night-pain of passion). Erotic desire can be all-consuming, lust can destroy, while love may tip to hate. At the time, celebrated poet Sappho dedicated her love letters to Aphrodite, mentioning that love is sweet and then bitter.

Ancient Rome picked up where Greece lost connection to the mighty Aphrodite. Merging her with their Venus, she was transformed into one of their most potent deities. She was back in business, and the elite claimed lineage to her, which might explain some of the excess, luxury and hedonism of the Romans. Examples abound – including the Emperor who smothered his unsuspecting guests in rose petals, or so the tabloids of the time tell it. Eventually, luxury was discouraged, and Venus became objectified. Pagan worship was outlawed as Christianity finally dominated politics and religion by the 4th century AD. In short, this deity came to us in a stripped-back version of a potent, prime and complex image. Thankfully we continue to morph Venus, ditching gendered stereotypes for a fresh take on an Ancient deity.

Venus – the archetype

Venus is an archetype of love and beauty. There may be highs, lows and fashions, but love is a permanent fixture in human experience. Venus permeates our world, turning up everywhere: in films, adverts, books, life. As historian Bettany Hughes says, 'Venus is still big box office!'.

Of keeping up with the Kardashian fame, Kim is a Venus-ruled Libran whose appeal is Venusian. She's expressing a current mainstream, and some may say patriarchally compliant, archetype of erotic love, beauty, desire and, of course, big bucks. Women have been saddled with a version of this archetype – being the object rather than the subject and expected to conform to specific types for a straight male gaze while boys are cut off from expressing their Venusian qualities. Thankfully, this is changing.

Social media provides a forum for a diverse range of expression. At the negative extreme it is problematic. However, there is good there too, in that more boys are exposed to what girls and women share, to new voices and perspectives, influencing them and helping them to identify and liberate this archetype in themselves. Conforming to strict gender lines is no longer relevant – and that's good news for Venus. By sharing our interests, experiences, images and words, we're further broadening the spectrum of this archetype through lived experience. As with all the archetypes, everyone has Venus in their chart and in transit.

Archetypes in astrology may be subverted but they can never be repressed. Love conquers all means Venus subdues Mars because we all need love, peace and harmony to live well. As the antidote to the rough side of Mars, when Venus wins, we live longer, healthier lives, seen, valued and appreciated for who we are in partnerships and social constellations.

Venus in transit on a collective level

As a fast-moving inner planet, collective experiences of Venus are fleeting but may show up when Venus is in aspect to outer planets. This may express through challenges to relationships, relationship harmony or even a swell in Venusian areas of the arts, design and beauty. Dating apps may see an uptick when Jupiter and Venus meet in the sky while humans meet up on Earth!

Venus in transit on a personal level

This is where the effects of Venus are felt – at the personal level.

Venus transiting the houses of your birth chart

Venus brings her principles of harmony, love and pleasure to the area of life each house represents. This is where you'll meet the archetype. According to the sign it's in, the Venusian archetype demands expression, so don't hold back; put yourself in the path of beauty, launch yourself into its arms!

Track when Venus the planet is passing through and actively look for a Venus presence in your life or dial up Venusian activity. Through your 1st House, you may appear more attractive and feel more sociable. Through your 5th House of romance and fun, why not add a few dates to your dance card, get creative, or lean into leisure activities. In the 6th House, you may meet a potential partner or Venusian type through your work, so make a date or go out for drinks with your work colleagues. It's time to jazz up your work area so you enjoy your time there. Since this is also the zone of mind/body health, it's time to pamper yourself! Luxury spa, massage or facial, anyone? Does Aries rule this zone? It might be time to step up your active gear to a luxury brand. Through your 11th House? Host a dinner party, accept invitations or hang out with Venusian friends doing Venusian things.

Venus transiting the natal planets of your birth chart

When Venus returns or forms a conjunction with your Sun (or ascendant), your attractor factor goes up. You're emanating the principles of beauty. Note the day in your calendar and see what responses you receive; that's the time to book that headshot. Again, the element and sign are vital to the kind of expression you'll experience or generate. In Water, it may be emotive music and emotional connectivity. In an Air sign, it may be invitations and talk time. Venus to inner planets has more effect than to outer planets. Venus conjunct your Moon may be a feel-good emotional connection. However, it won't have as much impact on your Pluto placement. Over your south node may mean it's not time to focus on relationships right now.

Planets transiting your natal Venus will activate your relationship and desire principle. The transiting Sun may highlight it as people become aware of your charm. If you work in a Venusian industry, your contribution may be recognized that week. Mercury may encourage you to communicate your desire. Pluto might push you into an obsessive take on love or draw out a consuming passion. With Uranus connecting to Venus, there may be separation or Uranian love interest. As always, combine the meaning of each planet involved and add the sign as flavour.

A challenging aspect to natal Venus, say a square from transiting Uranus, may represent a sudden separation that feels destabilizing, or perhaps it's you who needs to break away!

Work your Venus

Play with different styles and looks, don't get stuck on one thing. Amplify, tone down, direct energy into other expressions.

No matter where you are on the spectrum of identity, building or experimenting with your Venusian truths, it may be easier to step into a Venusian mode that's easily recognizable. But don't sell out your inner truth for the sake of external validation (although that's important too!). Venus spins in the opposite direction from the other planets; this is your chance to contribute and shape the world. Share your creativity as a tastemaker, lover and all-around expression of this marvellous and essential deity.

Personal challenges and Pitfalls of Venus

The glyph for Venus is also the symbol for female, so the qualities of Venus have been narrowed to represent what a good female is meant to be by a patriarchal society that defines you by your gender identity as opposed to, say, being human.

English is also a gendered language, making it trickier to navigate without perpetuating and reinforcing outdated gender stereotypes. Mercurial Lexicographer Erin McKean's quote, 'You don't owe prettiness to anyone ... Prettiness is not a rent you pay for occupying a space marked "female".' It inspired Florence Given's book title *Women Don't Owe You Pretty*. Artist and all-around modern woman, she's one of many raising consciousness about such age-old pitfalls.

In Ancient Greece, when the first full-sized, life-like nude of a Venus (a female nude) was created, it had the effect of disenchanting the goddess (and women) by seeing her as an object of desire rather than an embodiment of specific qualities. In her documentary *Venus Uncovered*, Bettany Hughes explains that it assumed a male

Astro Power

audience and cast her as a passive object with the viewer as the subject. There are too many tributaries from this point (scandalous in its day, although nude male sculptures were strewn about like wildflowers) to fit in this book. The shadow these times cast is long, dimming our experience today. Untangling our self-concept is like picking cat hair out of honey, but worth the effort.

Take away the gender bias

Ever-changing beauty standards are applied unevenly to women, pushing into a hyper-feminized ideal of what a woman is. Take the gender out of the Venusian archetype or see Venus as a boy to flip the script. Define the attributes of Venus and recognize how they express through many areas of life. And spot how, where and why they're repressed. Notice how you inadvertently support gender stereotyping through expectation or language, then refocus on the conceptual, not biological, qualities of Venus.

Self worth

Cosmetic surgery and extensive, expensive (time, focus and money) beauty regimes are major pitfalls of our era. It's one thing to enjoy, but Venus is equally internal; it's your relationship with yourself, your sense of truth and joy. Make sure you are doing it for yourself, not pleasing or catering to others unless it's two-way. What if you were to demand what is demanded of you? Turn things around when you feel put upon to provide the Venus element if it's out of alignment with how you feel or who you are. If someone (boss, partner, parent or culture) pressures you, tell them to deal with their own Venus or provide it themselves because yours is none of their business. You may really have to work your self-esteem, worth and value for this exercise, but it's empowering to experiment with. Role-play scenarios before testing on real-world pressures.

Issues around this may come up with a challenging aspect to your natal Venus. Your sense of self-worth is put to the test; a relationship or values may be tested in a cosmic game of jeopardy. Find the balance – watch for overdoing Venus in overspending, laziness, hedonism, excess or reliance on relationships that tip the scales on health and responsibility for your own destiny.

Venus retrograde

Because Venus is the brightest star, it has a central place in mythology for most cultures back through time. Essential to the Ancient Maya, they saw the morning star as a war deity and planned accordingly. In the first written epic poem is *The Descent of Innana*, correlating to the cycle of Venus. More of a chant or prayer, it follows the protagonist's journey through seven gates (seven conjunctions to the Moon), as she loses her worldly power, meets her shadow, dies, is reborn anew, then travels back through the gates to live again at full strength as the evening star.

The retrograde cycle of Venus is clothed in many a mythological tale and personification. Ancient Romans called the morning star phase Lucifer, Latin for 'the bringer of light', as it heralds sunrise. Eventually, the Latin name for the morning star and the retrograde portion of its cycle with the Sun (synodic cycle) was reconfigured via the Hebrew Bible as the Christian tale of a fallen angel called Lucifer, synonymous with the devil and evil. Another Christian correlation is the 40 (a number that appears repeatedly) days and nights Jesus spent wandering in the desert. Could this be based on the astronomical retrograde of Venus? If so, it aligns with the meaning of retrogrades: to reflect and touch base with your inner compass.

Venus conjuncts with the Moon seven times over the seven lunar months it takes to travel from the position of the evening star to visibility as the morning star.

Venus retrogrades about every 19 months, the least of all the planets, and it lasts for 40 days, completing a cycle and returning to the same point every eight years and going retrograde five times in its eight-year cycle.

In each retrograde cycle Venus conjuncts the Sun twice. It first passes the Sun, then on the retrograde it conjuncts again while passing the Sun. There are five conjunction points each way over the total eight-year period. Called star points, when tracing a line from one point to the next, they form a perfect five-pointed star. The pentagram is, therefore, a symbol representing Venus. The fractal-like geometric ratio in this cycle correlates to design principles of the golden mean and Fibonacci sequence. Greco-Romans used these design principles in their iconic architecture, sculpture and art. This pattern is present through nature from the nautilus shell to spiral galaxies.

This is a red alert over the Venus retrograde period, hex that ex. That road is lined with big red flags, avenues of them billowing in the wind. If this is you, here's your shout out: don't get back with a love zombie or turn into one.

Reflect on why the relationship didn't work and what compels you to go back there. The rule of thumb is not to move forward or begin anything new that is under the rulership of Venus, like starting a new relationship, buying a luxury item or radically changing your look. Retrogrades call us to move inward, while these are all external.

Conjunctions with the Moon

Over the retrograde period, Venus forms seven conjunctions with the waning crescent Moon. The number seven correlates to the spiritual number we see repeated in the seven major chakras, seven days a week, seven visible planets, and so on. The other planet of connection and love is the Moon, with its cycle split into quarterly seven-day phases.

Venus is invisible for 60 to 90 days as it passes the Sun; ascending from the morning star, it reappears as the sparkling evening star. Twinkling from this lofty height in the heavens, Venus is visible for 263 days. After reflection over the retrograde, by the time Venus has ascended, you've experienced another evolution in your maturity, insight and wisdom.

Venus out of bounds

Venus slips out of the Sun's bounds 12% of the time. Suggesting a period where love goes off-road into uncharted territory, beyond social norms and your own line, it sashays between acceptable and what was I thinking. However, this could be a great time to connect with someone you usually wouldn't. Push your artistic side into a new dimension or get perspective on a relationship that needs to either go or change. While Venus is unbound, insights into your desire nature may emerge along with awareness of social constructs you've been living within. The connection of Venus to money and spending may show up, so watch those impulse purchases that turn out to be outrageous or off the wall but seemed so wearable at the time. It's a little like shopping in an exotic country; it fits right in but just doesn't work when you get it home. Suppose Venus is OOB in the lead-up to holiday spending. In that case, it's a bumper season for retailers, especially when it's in Sagittarius! Went out for coffee, came home with luxury luggage!

The Visual Cycle of Venus

...and The Seven Lunar Gates
(Conjunctions)

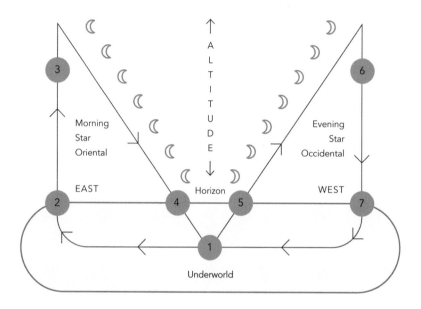

2. Heliacal Rise East   1. Interior Conjunction   5. Heliacal Rise West
3. Greatest Brilliance   6. Greatest Brilliance
4. Heliacal Set East   7. Heliacal Set West

The Dance of Venus

The orbit of Venus traces out a perfect five-petalled rose. Trace the star points of each conjunction with the sun to create a pentagram.

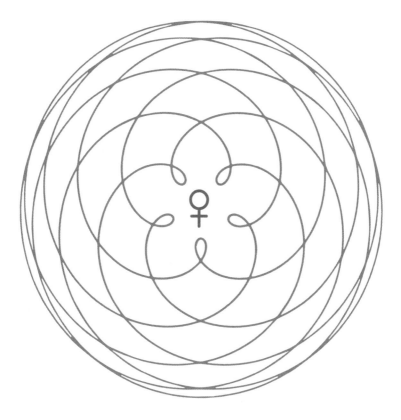

Mars

♂   # Mars

Carpe diem · Seize the day (Horace)

Keywords · Energy · Action · Will · Drive · Conflict · Assertive · Anger · Heat · Sex · Libido · Excitable · Strength · Courage · Bravery · Determination · Leadership · Initiative · Self-preservation · Bravado · Swagger

Orbit · 17–23.5 months; average 2 years

In a sign · 7 weeks–2 months; average 2 months

Rules · Aries

Functions well · In Aries, Scorpio and Capricorn

Take special care · In Libra and Cancer

Colours · Red and black

Crystals · Red, coral and carnelian

Metal · Iron

Function · Mars is the principle of assertion: to stand up for ourselves and go after what we want. It's the action principle. Represented by the sword or blade, Mars rules sharp metal that cuts or pierces, so it's about how you actively cut the cloth of your life, seize the day and your destiny. As the protagonist, you are the active doer rather than the passive receiver. Mars is self-oriented and one could say a necessarily selfish side that says, 'Get out of my way, I'm coming through!' It creates independence while also aligning with others towards a singular goal.

Since anger and rage cut and sever relationships, it can also be a driving force for change. As righteous anger, it tells you something's wrong and ignites the energy to do something about it. Mars provokes, stands up to or weathers conflict rather than backing down to keep the peace. It's the competitive impulse and combines with solar qualities in the will to live, with the drive and strength to do what it takes to succeed. Mars is ready to stand its ground or shove back.

Mars – the planet

> Known as the red planet due to its reddish hue, Mars isn't hot like the temper its astrological meaning suggests; it's freezing at minus 60°C (minus 76°F) with epic storms that can engulf the entire planet! With 62% less gravity, a dry, barren wasteland with no atmosphere, this is pretty much how Ancient Greeks saw their deity of war, Ares, and the land after Ares had laid waste to it.

Mars – the deity

The Greek Ares was the deity of war, a rough-hewn forebear of the Roman Mars. Ares represented the raw, primal and immoral side of violence. Although Greece had the usual soldiering, they didn't venerate Ares. They didn't build temples for him because inviting this deity was inviting death. Ares was distrusted and seen as having no allegiance, slaying the slayer in turn. Live by the sword, die by the sword.

The Romans, however, polished up those rough edges and eventually promoted Mars to protector of Rome, as Athena has been for Greek Athens. Mars represented a more disciplined side of this deity, bringing order and peacekeeping.

Identifying as a Martian people, the month of March is named after Mars, heralding the start of the campaign season on the 19th. This is also the beginning of Aries in the solar year. One of the attributes of Minerva, the Roman goddess of wisdom, was as a war deity. Eventually, she replaced Mars as the patron of the March festival. Campaigns ran biannually, matching the two-year planetary orbit of Mars.

Mars – the archetype

Mars is the archetype of warrior. The Roman soldier, the gladiator and the gladiatrix are all Mars. These days, the military is the obvious parallel, along with competitive sport, so members of the Forces and Olympians are classic archetypes.

The Olympic Games were first held in Ancient Greece. While women did not always compete in the same games, there were plenty of women rocking their Mars in athletics as girls were trained along with the boys by Crete, Sparta and the earlier Etruscans. The most Martian and successful city-state of the time, Sparta was more egalitarian. The first woman to win the games was Spartan, at a time when Greek women were excluded (from most social life) on penalty of death at catching a glimpse. Talk about jealously hoarding Mars. Inspired, more Spartan women went on to compete and win.

Today, top athletes are still challenging societal standards about women in sport. Men have no limit to testosterone or hormone levels, while women do. It's the same attempt at control around this archetype and gender, and like Mars, it's still a hot topic.

Ancient Greeks were obsessed with Amazons, not the least because women in Greece were so restricted. They were Scythian nomads, and tales of their abilities were reported as far as India and China. Referred to as the daughters of Ares (not a compliment at the time), they were mixed gender, as everyone was trained to ride, shoot a bow and handle weapons.

More recently, the all-female Agooji elite force in African Dahomey numbered up to 6,000 at their peak. Europeans who witnessed them in action reported they were superior in bravery and skill. After the French conquered, the army was no longer open to women, and they were forbidden to carry weapons. Always prepare so the backlash doesn't hit its mark!

Legendary Native American women fought to defend their people. Lozen, Dahteste and Buffalo Calf Road Woman, who delivered the blow that knocked General Custer off his horse, expressed the archetype of Mars full out. There are so many inspiring Mars archetypes that disprove the patriarchal narrative around women's identity and capabilities. Entrepreneurial women in business, like Cathy Wood, CEO and founder of Ark Invest are breaking ground. More women in politics are moving through the ranks to top jobs. The leadership aspect relies, in part, on the Martian archetype, which is one of the reasons there can be gendered push back. Patriarchy relies on women at the bottom, so a great way to flip it is to fulfil your destiny and go straight to the top!

The archetype is perhaps synthesized in the superhero, which has made a comeback over the last few years, with lots of new characters, and finally female-driven and directed. They're tough, fearless and leap in to save the day – super-Mars style.

Play 'spot Mars' and you'll see this archetype in more places. Make a Pinterest collection or mood board to open your mind and inspire you with images of strength and courage that you can call on when you need that extra Ka-POW!

Mars in transit on a collective level

Themes of Mars combine with those of the sign it's transiting through. In Air signs, the energy will be intellectual, perhaps inspiring debate or pursuing knowledge and comms. The altruistic side of Aquarius may direct focus and action onto humanitarian issues. In Water signs, acting on emotions, indirect action or creative pursuits come to the fore.

Forming an easy aspect to another planet, Mars may energize and motivate it to express externally. Trine Venus? Take action on a date, get to a gallery or actively mediate to a resolution. A challenging aspect could result in an argument that is difficult to resolve, requiring more work.

Mars in transit on a personal level

This is where the impact of the personal planets is felt most strongly.

Mars transiting the houses of your birth chart

As Mars moves through the houses of your birth chart, it energizes the relevant area of your life, so note your impulse to act or the direction you're moving in. Do you need to tweak it, change gear, assert or defend yourself? Strike out and blaze a fresh trail if it's in Aries. In your 7th House, it's better to get active with a partner to keep the energy moving rather than let it boil up or over. Watch for conflict and head it off by dealing with things head-on rather than indirectly. When Mars sets up residence in an area of your life, think about how you can channel the energy into the external world constructively rather than destructively.

Mars transiting the natal planets of your birth chart

Mars transiting inner planets will activate and energize them. The energy has to go somewhere, so be mindful if it's a challenging aspect, which is especially true of Mars combined with Pluto and Saturn. Step away from power struggles but don't be defeated. Be strategic and think about the war rather than the battle. Trine to your Sun amplifies the life force, willpower and helps you assert yourself in a way that supports your personality and direction.

Outer planets aspecting your natal Mars may show up as catalyzing energy, depleting energy or as an obstacle, depending on the traits of the planet and the aspect angle. Saturn in opposition results in rules or restrictions or someone with more authority than you. Will you scale the wall or back down? Transiting Saturn in a flowing trine to natal Mars lends strategy and endurance, focusing your energy on actions that last or step you up the ladder. It's an aspect of achievement, so what will you do over this time? How will you utilize it?

Work your Mars

Mars is the exclamation mark, the definitive movement at the right time, the kairos in Ancient Greek. You instinctively recognize an impulse to action. Like surfing a wave of cosmic energy or even catching a bus, if you miss it, it's gone. To be in the flow means moving with this energy, which requires a liberated Mars. Trust in this aspect of yourself, your inner knowing; acknowledge, accept and respect it. This is your instinct, saying 'Act now, seize the day!'

Call on Mars when it's time to put yourself first. Experiment: choose an awkward situation. Name what's going on and initiate the conversation, the action, the advance or the departure. When you control the frame, when you ask the questions, you're in the strategic position of control. Activate your Mars by keeping fit and active. Get your blood pumping and take up space with your body, voice, energy and ideas. Deal with obstacles, test your physicality, then everyday life challenges become easier to surmount.

Mars milestones – Mars return

We all have our first Mars return at two years old, something society is well aware of as the terrible twos! If you want to get a sense of Mars energy, try telling a two-year-old, 'no'. This is when baby humans test their will against yours. There's red-faced anger, screaming and no problem letting it all out. Every two years, we continue to experience a Mars return to its natal position in our chart, so watch the cycle and mark a calendar to catch yours. It's the beginning of a new cycle, so set out your intentions around how you want to use and direct your energy for the next two years. Be strategic around fitness, the building of strength and muscle, challenges and goals.

Personal challenges and pitfalls of Mars

As with so much gendered framing in astrology, the myth of Mars as male or masculine is among the strongest. But we all need to express assertiveness, anger, lust or the pursuit of our desires.

Over the last few thousand years, many cultures have gone to great lengths to establish these traits as male or masculine. But if women are allowed to get in touch with their softer side, how do they get in touch with their Mars? (And the opposite gender imbalance is also true!)

The pressure and messaging that only males must follow Mars can make it a tough call for women when they go for it, put themselves first, sweat or stand up to a challenge, but we are beating down the stereotypes. Mars is an energy, a principle, a part of every living creature. Gendering these traits is political, cultural, divisive and about power, not biology or astrology. Mars energy is primal; it's the outpouring of energy as part of life's cyclical ebb and flow.

Holding in anger turns to inflammation and imbalance; it stresses the body. Not pursuing your dreams crushes the spirit.

The biggest pitfall is simply not acting, not using your Mars or expressing your energy.

On the other side of the scale, the biggest pitfall for males can be living up to the social expectation of being all Mars and not acknowledging their emotional or creative potential. Pitfalls are the blind, destructive side of Mars as a release of frustration and anger as a cover to protect emotional vulnerability, perceived slights to an insecure ego and identity. You may feel your authenticity isn't acceptable and cover it up. Identify the source of your anger to find where the issue is. Reflection, therapy and a constructive outlet are all useful. Build a healthy relationship to your Mars principle and balance with the aspects of yourself.

Mars retrograde

Mars retrogrades every two years for two to three months per cycle. Since this is the planet of action, it's a great opportunity to reflect on your direction and how you're using your energy. Is it working, or could you learn some new approaches?

The area of your chart Mars will retrograde over is hosting this active principle for an extended run, so it's not business as usual. If planets or sensitive points are involved, this retrograde will be meaningful and perhaps show up as a need to redirect your energy, effort or approach. This is not the time to race ahead unless you've already done the work and attended to details.

Mars out of bounds of the Sun

When Mars goes out of range of the central organizing principle of the Sun, things could go awol or a tightly capped lid could finally burst free. If tension has been brewing, this may be the moment it catalyzes externally, especially if involved in a tense aspect set with other planets. In that case, use the energy to catapult you to a better situation or at least to get changes rolling.

This may be an empowering and energizing flight of fancy and adventure if Mars is well situated. Do or try things you wouldn't normally: take a different route to work or on your run, try a new yoga studio or gym. Unhinged and erratic are words used for OOB planets; in this case, watch sudden, reckless, impulsive actions.

The social planets

Jupiter · Saturn

For millennia these two giants were thought to be the outermost planets, so they indicated natural and social laws. Jupiter indicates luck and expanding your horizons, as well as aspirational ideals and beliefs. Saturn poses limits, restrictions and structure, but also the reality of tangible form. They're essential and useful astro ingredients; get to know their archetypes and harness them in service to your destiny.

Jupiter

♃ Jupiter

Maximus optimus · The biggest and the best
Keywords · Growth · Faith · Luck · Risk · Expansion · Abundance ·
Wheel of fortune · Enthusiasm · Joy · Knowledge · Truth · Philosophy ·
Natural laws · Large things · Allies · Higher mind · Goodwill · Justice ·
Excess · Ethics and morals · Fecundity
Orbit · 12 years
In a sign · 1 year
Rules · Sagittarius (and traditionally Pisces)
Functions well · In Sagittarius, Cancer (and traditionally Pisces)
Take special care · In Gemini, Capricorn (and traditionally Virgo)
Colours · Yellow, orange, gold, clear, bright, transparent colours
Crystals · Yellow sapphire, yellow topaz, citrine, yellow zircon
Metal · Tin
Function · Jupiter's primary function is growth. It expands topics according to
themes of the sign hosting it. At best it's called the monarch maker, crowning the
planet it comes into contact with, and elevating it according to, its own themes.

Call on Jupiter for opportunity, growth and faith. When you need the
universe to throw you a bone, dial into Jupiter!

Jupiter – the planet

Not to be outdone by diamond-bright Venus, Jupiter may be the
second brightest in the night sky, but it shines ALL night. Look up
and connect with Jupiter's light. The second largest celestial body,
Jupiter's sheer physical presence says it all: bigger is better!

That gargantuan red spot on Jupiter is a storm that has been
raging for centuries and reflects its namesake, who was a deity of
thunder and storms. Jupiter rules big things, and storms are the
biggest events of the skies, so naturally this deity had control of
them, reminding the people of their deity's power. Referred to as
the greater benefic or greater fortune in traditional astrology, let's
call it the great enabler because, like that red storm on the planet,
you'll be raging for centuries too with Jupiter as your party planner.

With its dominating size, Jupiter throws its gravitational weight around, tossing out comets and asteroids that get too close. It acts like a shield, taking one for the team so smaller planets like Earth aren't hit. No wonder the Romans looked up to Jupiter as the protector of their massive empire.

Just as Jupiter is so massive and can absorb space debris into itself, Rome's domination was born through unification and absorbing new cultures. They demanded the allegiance of village by village, growing mightier with each addition. The diversity of Rome's vast empire was a key to its success and reminds us of the strength of inclusion. Admittedly not everyone was equal or free, but this aspect of inclusivity reflects the archetype of Jupiter. The first globalists, citizenry was a winning strategy. Gaining that initial traction is the hardest part; once you've got it you attract more of the same. Like fame, or money, people give you more if you've already got some! When you have Jupiterian confidence in your abilities and your abundance, you're generous, and act along the principle of growth, fanning out in all directions. Even if you don't, give it a try and see how it makes you feel and how others respond. Like times of celebration and gift-giving, it makes you and others feel good, then others associate you with that great feeling.

Jupiter – the deity

Named after the most powerful of the Roman gods, Jupiter was adapted from the Greek god Zeus. Zeus has taken pole position from Hera, who preceded as supreme deity in earlier, more egalitarian goddess-centred cultures. However, Zeus was not always favoured throughout the populace, as Greece had an elite democracy with each town choosing its own featured deity. Rome's solo emperor mirrored Jupiter's takeover as number one across the vast empire. Perhaps Jupiter had a hand in uniting and strengthening the culture by reflecting an ideal, which brings us back to Jupiter's role as a social planet, linked with growth and cross-cultural expansion.

Zeus' mythological roots appear to be in Crete, although myths often tell stories based loosely on history, so they may well have begun as one of many Cretan clan deities. Migrating to Greece, Zeus's forerunner was absorbed into local culture, eventually finding fame, fortune and honour. In this tale of ascent is the spirit of this deity.

In myth, Jupiter overthrew their parent, Saturn, echoing themes of expansion past established limits or boundaries. If you're going to move past your comfort zone of your family, peer group, culture, ethnicity or gender norms, Jupiter is the deity to call on and channel.

If you're stuck or have come to the edge of your map ask yourself, 'What would Jupiter do?' The opener this archetype is made for is the question: 'what if …?'

Fill in the blank with a dream so outrageous you feel ridiculous, then write out at least twenty more what ifs. You're not committing just yet, so there's no pressure and no reason to back down from your biggest dream.

Jupiter – the archetype

Jupiter is like a powerful version of Santa Claus: generous, abundant and jovial. In fact, the word jovial comes to us from Jupiter, who was also known as Jove. Leaps of faith that optimism inspires takes Jupiter straight to the top while maintaining an only-good-vibes frequency. A bit like flying in a dream, it takes practice to push the clouds of doubt away and continue on your flight path. Channelling Jupiter's optimism will help you remain positive.

With a larger-than-life personality, optimistic things will work out. Jupiter goes for it, which takes an element of confidence, a bit of fake-it-till-you-make-it and a whole lot of not just self-belief but a belief that the universe is inherently good and will deliver your destiny. Jupiterian people are naturally abundant and often successful. If you attract a Jupiterian person into your life, they share opportunity and invest faith in you – you'll feel lucky you met them!

When you call in Jupiter, it may arrive as a teacher who embodies the archetypal qualities: perhaps an educator, someone with a company or larger operations behind them, a traveller or simply someone who in some way catalyzes you to expand your world.

Like all archetypes, what Jupiter represents shows up everywhere, especially in the drive to expand, due to the inherent principle of growth. Think large spaces, big things like Texas or the Himalayan mountains. Large media conglomerates, cruise ships, large buildings and long trips all come under the rulership of Jupiter. It doesn't mean they aren't problematic or necessarily about domination and excess, but it does mean there is a largess and scale about them. This is a social planet, so it rules the larger governing laws: of society, natural laws and religious laws or institutions (as opposed to direct mystic experience).

Jupiter as the monarch of the gods and its relationship to scale is one to note. When a ruler wanted to communicate their importance and cement their divine right to rule, who did they call on but Jupiter; those statues (of themselves), pyramids or other building works were super-sized in an effort to deify themselves in the minds of the people. So Jupiter may be the planet of exaggeration as well as over-compensation.

Jupiter in transit on a collective level

The sign, with its element and mode, hosting Jupiter indicates a one-year trend, favoured industries or areas along themes of that sign.

When Jupiter aspects or merges with another planet or planets in an easy flow, you know it will amplify the themes of that planet, according to the sign it's in, or add its upshift to the general mood of the time. When Jupiter was in Scorpio (sex, secrets, power) in 2017–18, the #metoo stories were bubbling up and women rallied together in support, so the issue was finally too big to put back in the bottle. Jupiter moved into Scorpio on 10 October 2017, and the Twitter hashtag was initiated on 16 October. Jupiter's jaws of life operating in Scorpio territory did us a collective favour. This is a charged topic that illustrates the buoyancy of Jupiter's application to it all the more. Since the orbits of the planets illustrate cycles and themes, the previous time Jupiter was in Scorpio was when the expression 'me too' was coined. Always check earlier cycles for a glimpse of themes to expect and the next evolution of those themes when you're looking ahead to time your destiny.

Jupiter in a sign

Like all planets, even Jupiter can do what it does best in some signs better than others. Certain signs are naturally geared towards expansion and faith rather than raw data or boundaries. This is why Jupiter finds affinity with Sagittarius, which it rules, and Pisces, which it ruled before the title was handed over to Neptune. The opposite sign of Sagittarius is Gemini, which wants to get to the point or simply chase random facts, and is less interested in overall meaning. Jupiter could increase the scattered nature of Gemini and end up with a wall of Post-it notes with no connection, so you may need to take special care not to endlessly seek data without boiling it down to a meaning and applying ethics. Alternatively, it could overdo meaning, blowing it out of proportion, which is a common pitfall of Jupiter.

Consider how you might express the archetypal themes of a sign in terms of Jupiter. How does the element of growth or luck express if it must act through the lens of a particular sign?

In Libra, the arts, beauty and perhaps law are all favoured. Teaming up may be more beneficial than a solo me-first approach this year.

In the opposite sign, Aries, you may activate Jupiter luck by striking out on your own, claiming leadership and blazing a new trail. Fresh ideas may be favoured and new ventures may be rewarded with attention and funding or a tail wind of personal confidence in your abilities.

Your Jupiter squad goals

Jupiter is associated with friendship, fellowship and alliances, while Jupiter's return coincides with new social and educational strata. Spending one year in each sign means the group you go through school with all share the same Jupiter sign, or one of two signs if it changed mid-year. That means you have a common thread around what optimizes you, sparks joy, where you put your faith and what your spirit grow lamp looks like. Anyone twelve, 24 and so on in approximately twelve-year increments will share the same Jupiter sign as you, resonate with you and could provide an element of collegiance, mentorship and inspiration around growth and encouragement.

Collective challenges of Jupiter

Unstable or unchecked growth leading to waste and overcommitment represent the flip side of collective Jupiter. Jupiter expands, but that doesn't always mean it has discretion. It may exaggerate a challenging combination of planets. Usually, its buoyancy is enough to raise anything from the depths, doldrums or neglected parts of society, but it can drill down a combination that is, by its nature, contracting, limiting or fearful – themes most of us want less of, not more. But Jupiter is here to provide more, so in this case it exaggerates contraction. An example would be a Jupiter, Saturn, Pluto conjunction in Capricorn, as experienced through 2020. Freedom and movement was severely restricted through closed borders and home quarantine, while fear of shortages partly drove shortages of some items.

Expansive Jupiter in aspect to a planet like Neptune, in a sign of no boundaries like Pisces, could function like aerosol and spread something you may prefer contained. It's all in the timing and the constellation of planets and signs, although Jupiter's role is always the same: to turn up the dial.

Elite Ancient Rome, perhaps spurred by the archetype they held highest, took the principle of excess to heart in long and lavish feasts. The vomitorium – where they vomited between courses to make room for the next – may be the shadow side of keeping up with Jupiter, not to mention a grumbly hangover the next day. Overdoing it with no limit for the sake of it is wasteful. An economic model based on unlimited growth and expansion lacks sustainability, so stay conscious of where you direct this impressive energy and be sure you can back up your commitments.

Jupiter in transit on a personal level

Firstly, Jupiter is a boon – it's hard to mess up with this one. You could sit back, relax and let the fish jump into your net, but you've still got to pull in that net and do the rest with your catch. At which point, Jupiter's job is done and the responsibility passes to Saturn. Or you actively could go with the theme of Jupiter and dial up the affairs of the house hosting it.

Jupiter transiting the houses of your birth chart

Since Jupiter is in a house of your birth chart for one year at a time, it's easy to track. By identifying the house it occupies and when, you can set goals and prepare to use the energies to your best advantage, and we look at a selection here. Opportunity is greatest when preparation meets luck after all. Why not follow it and dial up the affairs of the area of life it's moving through?

How could you offer your best to the deity? If you were going into the temple that Jupiter set up in that area of your life, how would you be the best devotee you could be – ultimately to your own purpose, soul and destiny?

Jupiter is about more, so why not try an experimental approach and keep expanding something until you reach an edge or limit. You may find there is none! And that may blow your mind. Most humans have psychological limits and if you've never passed a particular point, you may stop at this invisible boundary, a self-imposed glass ceiling, without even realizing.

The neural network we've developed mirrors our reality and we've spent our lifetime laying down those tracks, so be ready for some heavy lifting to get them to switch. Many people may even sabotage themselves to return to their comfort zone and to fit in. Sometimes others will try to bring you back. So be conscious about accepting the growing pains and confident you can step into bigger shoes and wear them comfortably. One of the biggest tricks to growth is simply accepting the changes ahead of time, as well as any fears around them. Identify and accept them and often that's the work done so they won't trip you up later.

1st House · Open up your perspective, look into your future with optimism and faith. Open up your sense of self. You may feel more robust and spot opportunities to set off on an adventure or do that thing you always wanted to do. Remember, there are always two sides to every planetary archetype, even Jupiter. You may overindulge and stress your body. This could be great for a body builder to draw on the title of *optimus maximus* – the biggest and the best – or go for a big personal challenge.

2nd House · Charge more, believe in your values and value yourself as well as your resources. This is a great placement for manifesting, so think big!

3rd House · Time to study something that sparks joy and expands your mind as well as opportunities later on: write, go on adventures locally or within your country.

10th House · Take the leap in career, call in the contacts or call up a mentor you'd otherwise think was out of your league. Jupiter is about hitting it out of the park – do that in your career! If opportunity comes knocking, open the door or go out and catch it yourself. If you're an influencer, grow your audience by showing up more over this period or launch a website to call followers over to your platform.

Ask yourself:
- What does Jupiter offer me and what is required of me to activate its gifts?
- How can I help the universe help me by aligning with the themes of Jupiter?

Remember the planet is what, the sign is how, and the temple is where.

Jupiter transiting the natal planets of your birth chart

When Jupiter transits a natal planet in your birth chart, you can apply the idea of growth, luck, faith and belief.

Conjunction · The result of Jupiter in conjunction with your natal planet is a merging and amplifying of the themes of that planet, with the result depending on the condition of the planet. If you are comfortable with growth, you will thrive. If you know you may need to prepare yourself, then get ahead of the curve and organize to incorporate and stabilize growth. Jupiter can 'release from bondage', according to traditional texts, so plan ahead on what that might be for you and how you can go about achieving it over this period.

Jupiter transiting your Sun · This is great for confidence, expanding your sense of self or identity. Luck comes through expressing yourself, your personality and, of course, having faith in yourself. Recognition is possible at this time, so put yourself out there and be seen.

Jupiter transiting your Venus · This could result in a lot of indulgence. Lap it up! Perhaps lots of relationships – why stick to one when Jupiter is in the house? – a larger-than-life romance or a Jupiter-type person entering your life. Luck comes through your values and your appreciation of beauty and worth, so cleave to them.

The trine · Similar to the conjunction, but the trine connects the affairs of two areas of life. It's easy growth and opportunity, so push for the maximum and make the most of your catch.

The square · This aspect can mean you overdo or underdo Jupiter's themes, sometimes overshooting or misjudging. Be sure to double check. You may not see an opportunity or know what to do with it, or you may have resistance to next levelling or growth.

Opposition · Jupiter opposite a planet could see you reaching further afield, but watch you get your measurements right. At oppositions, always make sure you are owning and integrating the archetype within yourself rather than projecting it onto someone else.

Jupiter in a sign

The theme of the sign is how you grow or ignite luck. Pisces is about belief, therefore dreaming up and believing in something are the first steps. Lean into your artistic and empathetic side.

Leo is about expressing your passion and creativity. For example, playing guitar sets up a frequency, dials you in and you attract more: more gigs if you're a performer, or more fans if you take action and upload onto a social platform.

In Capricorn it's your reputation that gets you everywhere. Taking on responsibility, commitment, aligning with a respected institution could be what makes you stand out from the crowd.

Work your Jupiter

Look at the theme of the sign, the element and mode hosting Jupiter in your birth chart. This is prime time to call in what you want and go for it as Jupiter's transit activates this point. Knowing this, check when your next Jupiter return is. Also spot when transiting Jupiter is going to be in the same element as your natal Jupiter or in the same element as your Sun, Moon or major configurations in your chart. This forms the most flowing and helpful aspect, the trine.

Jupiter's themes include release from constraint or bondage, as well as aligning the right conditions required for growth. Its manner is in the form of goodwill and is amassing as you go. Whether you want to leave a job or relationship, enter a new one, advance to the next level or simply go within and consult your inner archetype to ask the way, deliver your wish, or start a conversation of sorts and see what comes.

Generally when you begin school, Jupiter is half way through its first cycle and when you finish high school it is halfway through its second. Look back at your Jupiter cycle and write it up next to your timeline, then see which events correlate so you can have a better idea what to expect next time and plan ahead.

Pro-tool · Future time-lining is right up Jupiter's highway. Often we need to see it before we can be it. To grow into unfamiliar territory, you may need to lay down some new neural tracks in your mind before you step onto them in external reality. Visualizing yourself in your new reality, touch into how you want to feel, how it would feel to be that version of you. How would this person look, walk, talk and arrive? Don't think of practicalities at this point, just let your imagination create. Keep a check on ego inflation that may look to impress rather than authentically speak from your soul. Go for the inner feeling of warm, inspired upshift and expansion. If the inner feeling begins to shut down, note what the resistance is about. Have you hit the edge of your current belief around what could be possible for you? Is it realistic or have you found the edge of your conditioning? Check in with yourself; don't force the issue. Jupiter is about trust and good faith, so you must apply that to yourself as well.

Jupiter milestones – Jupiter return

Jupiter's return is your lucky year and it happens every twelve years. Like pouring fertilizer on an area of your life that already has a theme of more and abundance, this is your get-out-of-jail-free, jaws-of-life moment.

Even if you think you don't need it, Jupiter is here to say it's time to broaden your horizons, look at a larger perspective or go to the next level. Often this time coincides with your entry into the next level of education or society, while the opposition mark at six years ties into the story – we begin school at the first opposition at six and finish high school at the second opposition at 18.

The first Jupiter return marks the beginning of adolescence at age 12 and the beginning of high school. The second return at 24 is the beginning of young adulthood when you've most likely finished higher education. The third is mid-life at age 36. The fourth marks middle age at 48, the fifth is eldership at 60 and the sixth marks seniority at 72.

If you hit 84, then 96, you've really got the hang of Jupiter and quite likely sport a buoyant, forward-thinking mindset! Planting a garden and looking forward to its produce the following spring when you're approaching triple digits requires positivity and may fly in the face of the beliefs of both your relatives and society about what is possible and how it should look. Since Jupiter is about more, perhaps you can apply it to years and vitality. In studies on centenarians and very old people, this is something they all have in common.

Personal challenges and pitfalls of Jupiter

Sometimes you can get too much of a good thing, but Jupiter represents the greater fortune for a reason. Even the most tense aspect, the square, can express as extra energy, so you can rise to a challenge with more energy and enthusiasm than normal. An example is an Australian singer who had Jupiter square her Mars (energy and drive) at the time she was doing not one but two consecutive tours for her book with a spoken word performance and a final revival tour with her former band, all while taking time off from her career as a commercial pilot and launching an oracle deck.

If you have a Jupiter square or opposition coming up, it's fair warning to double check before you leap as you may misjudge the mark. If taking a risk, the benefit may fade once Jupiter has moved on, so be sure to do your due diligence and have a contingency plan. Apply this sensible advice for the temple of your natal chart Jupiter is passing through.

Don't be beguiled by a Jupiter-type person full of spin and promise. Also, be sure you can keep the promises you make, like keeping up repayments or coming through with the work you obtained.

Jupiter retrograde

Jupiter is retrograde (Rx) 30% of the time, so for four months each year, approximately 10° each year. It then moves forward about 40° achieving 30°, or one sign per year.

The principle of growth and expansion may slow and benefit from a review or recap. Don't push forward if it's not quite right; wait until Jupiter begins to move direct in the area of life represented by the (natal) temple hosting it. Since Jupiter is great at inflation and not so great at securing the foundations as it expands, these periods are beneficial, so runaway growth isn't left unchecked.

Saturn

♄   Saturn

Ad astra per aspera · Through adversity to the stars (Virgil)
Keywords · Principle of structure and order · Crystallization ·
Consolidation · Time · Limitation · Restriction · Separation · Walls ·
Discipline · Results through focus and work over time · Authenticity · Reality ·
Rules · Boundaries · Gravitas · Authority · Grit · Responsibility · Commitment ·
Mastery · Respect · Delayed gratification
Orbit · 29.5 years
In a sign · 2.5 years, that's 12° of a 30° sign per year
Rules · Capricorn (and traditionally Aquarius)
Functions well · In Libra, Capricorn (and traditionally Aquarius)
Take special care · In Aries, Cancer (and traditionally Leo)
Colours · Black, dark colours, brown, navy, grey
Crystals · Blue sapphire, black tourmaline, black onyx, pyrite, brown
agate, obsidian
Metal · Lead
Function · Like Jupiter, Saturn is a planet that governs society. It rules over
structures and hard, dense things like our skeletal system and teeth, as well
as bracing and support that may be applied to them: the reinforcing iron in a
skyscraper, the scaffolding needed while building to support it, training wheels
on a bicycle and perhaps the buckle on your belt. However, Saturn functions as
a polarity to Jupiter. Jupiter provides the expansion while Saturn provides the
complementary contraction for the eternal cycle of growth and decay, in and out
breath and contractions needed to birth life.

Saturn is the great teacher testing your limits through adversity to develop
resilience, character and authenticity.

Saturn – the planet

Beyoncé said it best: put a ring on it. Saturn's rings could be said to
represent the clear boundary marker that this planet is so famous
for. Commitment involves losing something to achieve something.
Try out Saturn by saying NO when you mean it and follow up with
some no-nonsense facial expression and body language so your
message is clear. Early meme sensation Grumpy Cat has plenty of

     Astro Power

Saturnian inspo on how to say no and why it's great – if you frown, other people leave you alone and you don't have to do anything. No. Saturn is anything but a people pleaser.

The final visible planet for millennia, Saturn's archetype is built around observation of the planets, its position in the stellar line up, and even its quality of light. It was furthest away, hence isolation. It was the final one, so we gain meaning around absolute finality and death. And it twinkles a dull brown, implying that the buck stops here, as it gives off sombre, end-of-the-road vibes.

Saturn slows things down, representing things that take a long time. They may be things you become known for since it had the longest orbital time.

Saturn – the deity

In Greek mythology, Chronos represented the devouring nature of time, in the end reducing everything to dust. Its nature is cold and dry while its function is to separate and isolate – perhaps to finally separate us from our illusion that we are solid, from our love affair with the material world.

However, since we're here, this hard-line material girl best exemplifies the title from Ru Paul's song 'You better work!' and Britney Spears' 'You want a hot body? You want a Bugatti? You want a Maserati? You better work, bish. You want a Lamborghini? Sip martinis? Look hot in a bikini? You better work, bish.' If you want the spoils and earthly delights, you're going to have to go out and get them unless you were born with the proverbial silver spoon. It all sounds so materialistic, but that's the realm of Saturn: status, achievement, respect from society. So, can Saturn be spiritual? Ultimately, perhaps Saturn gives us cause to look for more.

Saturn is the time lord slowly withering our skin, so it dries, tightens and peels away to reveal and release our true nature and glowing soul within.

Saturn comes to us from a mix of deities. One aspect is an agricultural deity, doing the less glamorous work behind the scenes, tilling and preparing fields, then collecting the harvest with the scythe. The saying 'You reap what you sow' is 100% Saturn. The scythe also represents the cold, hard conclusion; the definitive yes or no; the end.

Saturn represents the Establishment, those traditionally holding power, like the government and traditions belonging to it. The control they have is housed under Saturn, as are the systems and structures that keep the Establishment in place. The way things have always been done, sometimes beyond living memory, perhaps for generations, is Saturn's domain. The caveat Saturn reminds us of is that we live in a vast system that may or may not privilege us to varying degrees. We have room to move within that, but you can't positive-think yourself out of the wider social structures. So don't feel Saturnine guilt about that. Do what you can within the reality of constraint and opportunity.

Saturn – the archetype

While Saturn is essentially serious, each archetype has its own type of humour – gallows best describes this dry wit. Celebrating life with a reminder of death with the artistic and symbolic *memento mori* is a sobering reminder to feast on life!

Estée Lauder once said, 'I never dreamt about success, I worked for it.' With Saturn, it's all about authority, gravitas and maturity. Saturn is the silver-haired CEO who knows every nook and cranny of the biz by making her way up the ranks, a stern teacher that you're thankful held you to task. There's no enabling with Saturn; what you have, you earned.

Where Jupiter represents beliefs and faith, Saturn comes along to test your faith or philosophy. If you believe in something, this is where the rubber hits the road. Are you willing to put the work, sweat and tears behind it? This is the arduous, time-consuming side of manifesting in our dense material reality.

Saturn represents what it takes for anything to become old: time. The clock ticks slowly through the hours. What you do with those hours is entirely up to you. And what you have in the end is entirely up to you too.

People in uniform represent the authority of the state or nation, so while they may not personally express a Saturnian archetype, they do by proxy once they put on their uniform, hence strict code-of-conduct rules. If you have authority issues, people in positions of authority will capture your projection because you may be responding to your inner relationship with the archetype, not the person.

Saturn is the wise grandparent and although Saturn was often represented as a paternal archetype, there's no gender to wisdom. That gendered image was based on a patriarchally enforced situation banning women from any positions of authority, whether in households, professions, businesses, universities, states and countries or officially influencing the system that kept them bound. That said, for a classic Saturnian look, recall Abraham Lincoln. His face says it all! Gothic, solemn and severe, with the weight of the world on his shoulders.

Find your own representations and create a vision board or Pinterest collection to reflect the concept with a relatable and aspirational character.

Saturn in transit on a collective level

As Saturn takes 2.5 years to go through each sign it's still moving relatively fast. However, that's 29.5 years to return to the same spot. Themes from the previous cycle may reveal what to expect this time around.

Saturn in a sign

Since Saturn is about structure, the themes and areas belonging to the sign hosting it may become a focus, perhaps a push to make tangible rules, undergo limitation or be taken more seriously.

Saturn in Aquarius · Community and humanitarian concerns come into focus, putting social justice on the map and demanding that the rules be changed. Saturn was in Aquarius as the people of Los Angeles protested for human rights and safety in 1994, sparked by the murder of Rodney King. History repeated itself on the next transit through Aquarius in 2020, sparked by the murder of George Floyd. Both were about the abuse of authority invested in police professionals against the African American community. The hashtag #Icantbreathe further summed up the element of Air (Aquarius is an Air sign), and the restriction of it (Saturn). These were weighty topics well overdue for expression, as Saturn is nothing if not serious and sombre. We can expect a reprise at the next Saturn return if these issues aren't dealt with.

Your Saturn squad goals

Your Saturn squad is an age bracket of 2.5 years. If you had friends either side of your year at school, this may be a contributing factor. You're here to share the responsibility highlighted by the sign your Saturn placement shares. Your comrades understand the struggle is real. Find your crew and work through your Saturn challenge according to the sign it is in.

Saturn in transit on a personal level

Saturn is about building your own set of standards, your personal sense of authority, approval rating and validation. Wherever Saturn is transiting in your chart is where issues around Saturn's topics may be exposed, giving you the opportunity to correct them. You have the chance to align with your authenticity in a way that will set you up over the long term.

Saturn transiting the houses of your birth chart

Saturn, as it moves through the houses of your birth chart, indicates the areas of your life most affected by its themes.

The saying, 'your star is rising' refers to the transit of Saturn as it rises to the top of your chart. You may still encounter doubt or testing obstacles, but don't let them deter you; keep striving towards your dream. For inspiration, think of mountain goats scaling sheer cliffs or find images of your own.

1st House · When Saturn moves across your ascendant into the first house, this can feel like a mini-identity crisis. The zone of the self and outlook are up for restructuring. At this point, discipline comes easier, so embrace the opportunity to focus if things have fallen away or you feel a little more isolated than usual. As Saturn moves down to the bottom of the chart, there may not be much happening on the surface and this can be described as the long, dark night of the soul. There may be soul-searching as you sail through Saturn's doldrums, but the seeds of your success have already been sown. At this point the work you do will pay off later, so till those fertile fields!

7th House · Once Saturn reaches the 7th House cusp, it has surfaced onto the horizon and can be seen. Things are looking up! From this point, it makes the climb towards the top of the chart, and you should be seeing some results. Keep going, don't slack off!

This is where transiting Saturn was in Barack Obama's chart when he announced his run for presidency, later becoming President of the USA. He appeared like a new dawn, but he'd already worked for years.

In the 7th House of relationships, you may become committed to something longer term, so choose wisely. You may think more seriously about partnerships, attract an older, conservative or established person representing Saturn, feel the brunt of isolation in relationships or decide to be more self-sufficient. Saturn here may give you the opportunity to establish necessary boundaries.

10th House · It takes years to become an overnight success. Once Saturn reaches your 10th House of career, the highest point of your birth chart, your star has officially risen. What you do is noticed, and what you're into – your business or expertise – is just what people want. You may meet influential and well-connected people and be taken seriously. You can cruise through and watch things work out a little better than usual, or you can make the most of it by thinking long term, building on and securing your progress. Channel Saturn by owning your authority, acting responsibly and making tangible moves that matter.

The cosmic clock is always right on time. Transiting Saturn moved out of Obama's 10th House of career a few days after he stepped down from the top job.

Saturn transiting the natal planets of your birth chart

On the positive side, Saturn may focus and consolidate the function of a natal planet according to its situation by sign, house and aspect. For example, Saturn conjunct the Sun. You may feel less able to express yourself in a light way, however, apply your creative talent to something tangible. Nose to the grindstone! The isolation of Saturn can be apparent, but Saturn correlates to cutting out distraction and fluff, so you may as well immerse.

In a square aspect, you may overdo Saturn by taking on too much responsibility, feeling depressed, isolated or underdo by avoiding the call to step into responsibility. Instead, you may be blindsided by responsibility or limitation heaped onto you. Will you take up the call? Note if you're feeling overshadowed by someone else and work to shine bright. Life may be behind the scenes for this period, so plan your big comeback!

In opposition, Saturn may be seen as a wall or obstacle, with authority making the rules. Someone else is the authority pushing you to step up and own it yourself. Don't just give it away, apply gravitas and boss up already.

Work your Saturn

Own your authority, wisdom and experience. You worked for it!

While social apps and being online can be a great way to connect and for some a heady business tool, they do drain focus, creativity and attention with the lure of immediate gratification. Saturn demands solitude for deep work. This is where the isolation associated with Saturn is well placed. Make decisions and choices that put your time towards a longer-term ambition or goal. Say yes to projects that have a solid outcome and no to time-wasters that leave you with nothing of substance.

Ask yourself, 'what would Saturn do?' What is my long-term plan and outcome? What do I need to do to achieve it? Does this decision or use of my time take me towards my goal? How am I representing myself?

Embrace your authority

For some time, many positions and perceptions of respect and authority were closed to women who, in earlier cultures, had once dominated them. We've come a long way, but when you think of the archetype of say, a professor, you may still think of an older, bearded, bespectacled man. Mary Beard, a world-renowned professor, says it's essential we create new ideas around what authority is and break down false beliefs that continue to disable woman's claim to status and respect. For example, the image of a professor or the authority of a higher voice versus a lower one is infused with gender-based disinformation. Studies show it makes no difference, it's only the bias we've been socialized with that's informing our perception. It's important to raise consciousness on these pitfalls if you're going to step into Saturn. Rather than mould yourself to fit an outdated social concept, mould the ideal to fit you as it serves more people in the end, and Saturn is all about carving out an enduring legacy.

Combat ageism

Ageing is ruled by Saturn, but so is the wisdom and benefits that take a long time to accomplish, like success and status. Women are better served by respecting our path rather than allowing ourselves to be dismissed or dismiss ourselves at any age, especially as we enter our wise years. Embrace your age, show up and represent or you'll be missing out on the benefits of Saturn. Be proud no matter where you are on the timeline and never apologize or put yourself down for it. Remember, it's all a matter of perspective. Think of someone very old and how they perceive you. A 95-year-old looks at a 50-year-old like spring chicken, a 30-year-old as being wet around the gills and a 20-year-old as still pecking its way out of the shell!

Saturn milestones – Saturn returns

Adulting age 29.5 years · The first Saturn return is one of the best-known astro milestones. Like all transits, its effects depend on the arrangement of your birth chart, however, there are themes that we can all relate to. And with Saturn, that's maturity and taking on responsibility. The folly of youth is over; this is your adulting moment, the point where you step into your own.

Work with Saturn and embrace the focus this transit can deliver. Let go of your parents' expectations and step into your heart's call to destiny. Some people go back to study what they really wanted after putting in the years making their family happy doing what they 'should' do, not what they knew they wanted. Others may step into more authority in their career, marry, have a child or buy their own home.

Seniority age 59–60 years · Saturn makes a comeback at 59 for the second return. I like to think of it as the second coming, reminding you there's another life waiting. Build on the foundation of this one, become a master at what you do, step into consultancy or move into a new area. It coincides with a Jupiter return, so it's bouncier than you might think. Ask people older than you what they did around this age to get an idea of the variety of ways it can be expressed.

Eldership age 88 years · The third Saturn return pulls in at the ripe age of 88. If you're still kicking by this age you're literally etched with the wealth of wisdom you've gained through life experience and hard-won lessons. The inner substance and spiritual life is key as you turn towards an inward structure, reflect on and let go of the past.

Personal challenges and pitfalls of Saturn

Saturn has a long list of what most people would regard as undesirable potentials: from pessimism to distrust, austerity to isolation. Every planet can't represent love, light and unicorns, however, each planetary archetype has its path to your ultimate destiny. Life is tough but so are you.

While experiences or psychological processes that carry the Saturnian archetype can be a cross to bear, at least you're expecting it when you know how to time your transits. Saturn rules the metal lead, its nature is naturally dense and heavy. Saturnian types get on best when the going gets tough, because it doesn't take them by surprise and their inner fortitude activates. They're at an advantage because they know scaling heights is quite the reverse of cruising down a water slide. This is a sign of achievement through your own endeavours and, like Saturn the reaper, you reap exactly what you sow.

The challenging side of Saturn can include themes of fear, loneliness, depression and grief. Saturn isn't a fun planet, but what you put in you get out so wherever Saturn appears, hard work and discipline often reward. Other ways Saturnian themes can show up are around the basic idea of contraction and limitation. The more spiritual or mystical resources you have to dig into the better if existential crisis is on the menu. If depression rears, get guidance from an expert to lift the heavy lid on what emotions lie beneath it. All emotions must be faced, felt and in some way that part of the self must be loved, or at least accepted, in order to set it free. Things can't be forced and with Saturn, they may take time.

Check the date Saturn will move out of a difficult position (such as square your Moon) so you can see the light at the end of the tunnel. The saying 'this too will change' will help fortify you and remind you to take advantage of any trials and work diligently to deal with an obstacle while it presents. This way you're in a better position once you arrive at the easy aspects.

Saturn retrograde

Saturn is Rx for 4.5 months annually, that's 36% of the time and approximately 7° annually. It moves forward about 10–16° annually.

When Saturn is retrograde your long-term plans in the house it is occupying may grind to a halt and you may question them. For example, in the 10th House of career, you may question your direction, drop the momentum or ball you were running with to reflect on what you're doing or how you're doing it. Once Saturn moves direct again you may implement the changes you needed and move forward. Like all retrogrades this is a natural part of the inhalation and exhalation needed for life. In this case it's to maintain a solid structure, authenticity and alignment with your principles. Since Saturn spends so much time in retrograde, it isn't necessarily something to sweat, but worth a mention to avoid frustration.

The bridge

Chiron

Chiron stands alone as a bridge between Saturn, the old world, and Uranus, the new school. Not an easy position to be in as these worlds don't always go together, just like Chiron in myth. Chiron is our link between the tangible known and the unknowable future, our body and our ability to reach for the stars spiritually. It's the wound where these two worlds meet and how to heal by contributing from that space.

Chiron

♀ Chiron

Medicos et oraculi · Healer and mentor
Keywords · Shamanic · Wounded healer · Mentor · Foster care ·
Core wound · Abandonment · Like cures like
Orbit · 50 years
In a sign · 1.6–8.33 years
Function · The maxim 'healer, heal thyself' might as well be about Chiron. Called the wounded healer by astrologer Melanie Reinhart, Chiron points to a place we are wounded, even if we don't realize it. Remaining a sore or sensitive spot, it instigates our healing journey and, on the path to healing ourselves, we learn skills that will enable us to spot the same pain or dilemma in others and offer help. As in the homeopathic approach of like cures like, the talents or skills can be found in the wound if we're willing to take the journey to unfold them.

Themes of abandonment, not belonging, rejection, orphanage, fostering and mentorship are bound up in the meaning of Chiron. Its function may rely on separation, detachment and an objective viewpoint.

The Japanese art of Kintsugi, golden joinery, is often used to describe how something can be exquisite even after it has been damaged, depending on what you do with it, which is a beautiful analogy for the heart and soul development Chiron offers. Rumi, the 13th-century mystic, said it best: 'Don't turn away. Keep your gaze on the bandaged place. That's where the light enters you.'

While we should be careful of falling into a trap of suffering for our spirituality, we do ebb and flow. On the ebbs, we gain wisdom and a measure of enlightenment and often a sense of our destiny. This is where the light shines out as well.

Chiron – the planet

Astronomers can't quite define or agree on what Chiron is. Not quite a comet, asteroid or planet, it's currently a large asteroid and a minor planet. Not quite one of the centaurs of the Kuiper belt either, it runs its own elliptical route between Saturn and Uranus, just crossing their orbits. For our purposes, let's call it a planet. Discovered in 1977, it has only been in our astrology and consciousness for a comparatively short period of time.

Chiron – the deity

We don't have millennia of carefully recorded astrological observation on Chiron, however, we do have the Ancients' concepts embedded in mythology. To Ancient Greeks, Chiron was the product of dalliance, with some shapeshifting thrown in. When baby Chiron was born as a chimera – part human, part horse – their parents were unimpressed and Chiron was promptly abandoned. This gives rise to the themes of rejection and abandonment: since Chiron was abandoned, they felt unacceptable. The Greek version of Chiron wasn't a regular human nor a regular centaur, so didn't fit in anywhere. Not fitting in may show up in both natal Chiron placements as well as by transit.

As luck would have it, Chiron was found, fostered and taught an enviable and extensive curriculum from healing to hunting. Mature Chiron set up the Chironium, a healing sanctuary out of town in Mount Pelion, and, in myth, mentored all the heroes we're familiar with. This tale is symbolic of the collected knowledge and wisdom in maturity, and the suffering along the way. In images, Chiron is always depicted as older.

Chiron was a gifted healer, understanding natural medicine. However, Chiron was accidentally shot with a poisoned arrow. In excruciating pain, Chiron petitioned Zeus to renounce their immortality in return for the freedom of Prometheus – who at the time was chained to a rock in agony. Zeus agreed and Chiron was transformed into the constellation Centaurus.

The glyph for Chiron looks like a key, and this act of transcendence is a key to the meaning of Chiron's tale. Wounded both at birth and as an adult, Chiron transcended pain by helping someone else. In the myth, Chiron was transformed into a constellation, linking their destiny to a higher purpose.

Chiron's obit from Saturn out to Uranus suggests moving out to an unknown, higher realm outside the pain of living, taking it to a transcendent place, then looping that knowledge back as Chiron travels in to cross Saturn's orbit. It's an elevation of awareness or consciousness; it's visceral, a knowing in every cell.

Chiron – the archetype

Shamanism, indigenous knowledge, natural healing and plant medicine have gained ground over the past years. These represent Chiron well as they explore wounding and trauma in a search to understand, heal and transcend rather than medicate or suppress symptoms. Searching out the underlying emotional, energetic, psychological or even ancestral influences involves the kind of shapeshifting Chiron's human/centaur body represents. Ordinary waking reality doesn't always hold the key. Some traditions require a trainee to learn directly from the plants and forests through altered states. Western allopathic medicine is proving not to be a cure-all, while the system groans under pressure of dis-ease and cost. As people experience the benefits of other possibilities, they're sharing knowledge, stepping into the next stage of their Chironic journey and training others.

Chiron in transit on a collective level

Forecasting with Chiron helps shed light on themes around some of the challenges in our past, present and future. They are, by nature, painful and will be obvious throughout the collective.

Chiron in a sign

Due to Chiron's elliptical orbit, some signs host for several years while others are fleeting.

Years in each sign · Aries 8.33 · Taurus 6.93 · Gemini 4.46 · Cancer 3.09 · Leo 2.23 · Virgo 1.83 · Libra 1.66 · Scorpio 1.96 · Sagittarius 2.6 · Capricorn 3.56 · Aquarius 5.48 · Pisces 7.83

Rulership · Being relatively recently discovered, Chiron doesn't have any sign affiliations or rulerships, which is fitting for the planet that rules not belonging, the maverick.

Chiron in Pisces · Themes of the sign hosting Chiron is where we experience pain and wounding, highlighting it, triggering us to deal with it. The day Chiron moved into Pisces in 2010, the largest oil spill in history occurred through marine drilling. The wide diffusion of the oil over the ocean combines with wounding, (Chiron) and the Pisces element, the sea and liquids.

Chiron in Aries · This occurs from 2018–2027 so issues around independent action, fire or heat, weapons, fighting and perhaps the head (Aries rules the head) are on the table. So far, we've had unprecedented fires in the Amazon, Australia and California. Global warming is becoming more apparent with record-breaking temperatures. The wound is exposed and we must heal it.

Aries is all about the individual and identity, and while things have been expanding around gender identity, backlash has begun as it exposes such a raw nerve in how our society is constructed. That raw nerve is all Chiron.

The wounded warrior is a classic combination. Perhaps exposure to war means we see its reality. The last time Chiron was in Aries was 1968–1976, when we witnessed huge protests as Americans called for the Vietnam war to end. This time around, issues with fuel, cars, guns or violence – all Aries themes – may peak and hopefully be dealt with.

People who need the most healing around Aries themes are women because Aries energy has been denied them. Around the world we're seeing more women speak up and protest for their civil rights. Awareness of personal or individual trauma around violence and repression has been highlighted.

Chiron in Taurus · Once Chiron moves into Taurus in 2027, the Earth, the environment, food/food production, our body and senses, values and perhaps money will be the ground for triggering and healing. Last time Chiron was in Taurus, the cost of new technology further divided the have and have-nots. It may do so again.

Your Chiron squad goals

Not all Chiron squads are equal since the transit through some signs is so short the issues don't take as long to set in. It also means you don't have the benefit of a generation to understand your shared pain; the window is much smaller, so you'll have to narrow in on your crew. People with Chiron in the same sign for several years come up through a period when the issues have time to either resolve or develop. They also become a generalized backdrop you won't see so clearly until Chriron has moved on to a different sign. Understanding your squad's pain point means you can share with other people that have a similar issue and bring your efforts into the world consciously.

Chiron in transit on a personal level

If you have Chiron well placed in your birth chart it won't ping as much as a compromised position, such as a square or conjunct your natal Moon. Chiron moves slowly, but it will move on – hang in there and you'll be the wiser for it.

Chiron transiting the houses of your birth chart

The house hosting Chiron is where you'll meet this archetype and may be called to face a few painful truths or go through an experience that leaves you wiser and more empathetic. Chiron can be a heart opener, so throw your heart wide open but always be sure to apply boundaries. Respectfully leave an environment if it's toxic. Don't try to do self-development work to make someone else's behaviour more acceptable – that's their job. Just consider why you have allowed the situation to develop.

This is the area of life you may meet a mentor, or realize you're ready to become one, no matter how informal or formal the arrangement. Perhaps it's time to impart your wisdom.

6th House · Chiron through this area may show up as a physical imbalance. Not necessarily serious, but if you repeatedly get a sore throat you really need to reflect on what you need to express, and why you aren't. Louise Hays' book, *You Can Heal Your Life* is your go-to. It will get you rolling on the underlying emotional causes of physical symptoms. This is an excellent time to pursue training or work that touches on the themes of the sign Chiron is in while in your 6th House. You may deal with healing or wounded people through your work, or be the one feeling pain. Is it time to change jobs and pursue your destiny?

7th House · Chiron is met through the partner or one-on-one. When Chiron travels through the house of partnerships don't try to look after wounded birds and don't even think about dating them! Deal with them as clients so you work with this archetype but it doesn't affect your personal life. Wounding may be felt through a partner's trials and tribulations, or a health crisis, or they may trigger a sensitive point in you. You'll need to work out if they are just a catalyst, if you need to heal your own issue, or if they aren't right and need to go.

11th House · You may be ready to mentor in a group or in some way be involved with your peers. The sign Chiron is in will determine the themes. On the other hand, you may feel the sting of rejection, not fitting in or feeling misunderstood through your social activities.

Chiron transiting the natal planets of your birth chart

Square Venus · This could be experienced as wounding via a relationship, desire, around your values, your look or beauty. It will make or break a relationship, so let it go if it wants to go. If you're clinging to a wounded person in a relationship because you think you can heal them, think again.

Trine Sun · This easy aspect suggests healing to your identity and sense of self is smooth. You're perceptive to issues around self-esteem, projecting personality and confidence. You may be able to express yourself with more sensitivity at this time and naturally mentor by expressing your solar self.

Work your Chiron

Ask around and try out different healing techniques to see which work for you. The best are often the most simple, intuitive and inexpensive, so don't think you have to buy your way out. Try EFT tapping or self-hypnosis. Defragg your nervous system with meditation; cleanse from digital devices. If your wound is deep, assisted therapies for deep trauma and PTSD/CPTSD are getting great results. Study or develop your unique mix, share your healing wisdom, find a mentor or become one yourself.

Chiron milestones – Chiron returns

The Chiron cycle will most likely build on your natal placement and unfold over the course of a 49–51-year cycle. This is a journey of development; it's impossible to know or understand the end before you get there because you're creating it as you go. You may be soul-searching, but it will be worth it in the end. Enjoy times of solitude, go within as the universe/your higher self has cleared your schedule so you can. It can be easier to sense your destiny in the stillness, not when the world is buzzing at your door. But move on when it's time and build your life authentically.

Waxing square 5–23 · This may be a crisis point where Chiron's themes are felt. The nature of your wounding becomes clear and you must find a way to shift into the next phase. This is a period of growth, even if it's unpleasant, and may be rewarding in the end. Again, your natal placement dictates the severity. You may find you switch peer groups, are new in town or have to push into a new area.

Opposition 12–37 · Here we're faced with a Chironic situation: someone triggers your core wound, perhaps not on purpose. You may experience it through another person who is struggling with their own core wounding, perhaps a partner or close friend. Oppositions are a mirror and they reveal the truth. What is the truth you can learn? Always look for mentors, friends and authentic experiences; let go of anything that is not right for you.

Waning square 26–44 · If you've been tracking the hard angles of your transit, you know the theme by now. If you don't, you'll recognize it now as an unfoldment of the journey so far. Themes are most likely to repeat if you haven't tackled them. Use your healing strategies and be kind to yourself.

Chiron returns · The Chiron return is a homecoming 50 years in the making. You've run the entire course and you know it by now. Perhaps you recognize that old feeling and simply welcome it, are able to sit with it in yourself or others. You are the mentor.

On average, the menstrual cycle ends at the Chiron return, so it's an entry into the next stage biologically for half the population. Leading up to it, a major process of biological alchemy has or still is taking place, heating up, transforming from the fire within. Astrologer Barbara Hand Clow calls Chiron the 'rainbow bridge' because it bridges between Saturn and Uranus. I'd say this is your rainbow bridge moment. You may feel anger at all that you've dealt with as you're not willing to put up with behaviour or treatment you let slide before. Use that anger as fuel to make the changes you need to, or stand up for others. This could be your angry moment – feel it!

Because life is a cycle, the way you entered menarche, the attitudes, the way you've looked after your body, all come home to roost now. You may need to work through a few things, then put them on the bonfire and let them burn. If you're young and reading this, take note and embrace your changes all the way through. Everyone moves into 50, if we're lucky enough to make it, and we all evolve through this change in one way or another.

This is like the autumn years; it's moving into a decade of peak professional development and time to truly share your accumulated wealth. The Japanese call it the second spring, because you live for you now (even more if you already did!). This is part of the Uranian influence on liberation. It's a becoming, best celebrated, with a positive perspective. Most literature about this period of life takes a depressing angle, but don't believe the patriarchal hype, it's an exciting and transformative stage in your developmental process.

People over 50, especially women, say they stopped caring what people thought and finally did what they wanted. To me, this echoes the myth of Chiron and Prometheus. At the return you've gone one full round and choose to transcend rather than stay in the same pain. Ultimately the pain during a Chiron transit may be searing enough to finally face it, come to terms with it and let it go; respond to your higher calling. This is your Prometheus moment. You're ready to fly.

Personal challenges and pitfalls of Chiron

Where we perceive a wound, we may inadvertently project it, creating a self-fulfilling prophecy. If you experience the theme of abandonment, check in on whether you have just abandoned yourself or been instrumental in that happening. If so, ask yourself when you last felt the same way. Keep an attitude of interested curiosity and suspend judgement. Does a memory, scenario or person pop into your mind? How is that situation like this one? Check the transits for that time. This gives you a solid place to start.

In the end, self-acceptance is the key. It doesn't mean you can't change but accepting yourself here and now is healing.

Chiron retrograde

Chiron moves back and forth, sometimes retrograding over one point up to five times. At its slowest in Aries, it can take up to 19 months just to get past one degree.

If you have a transit to a sensitive point like your Sun, Moon or ascendant, write out the dates it will be in orb, very close, exact and then moving on. Themes begin to set up as the orb tightens. Around exact, you're in the zap zone, and you may get a few repeats on the theme as it reverses over the planet or point a few more times. Take note of the themes unfolding and be gentle with yourself over this period if there's nothing else you can do. If it's not hitting any particular points, there will be bigger headlines, so don't focus too much on Chiron.

The outer or transpersonal planets

Uranus · Neptune · Pluto

Uranus, Neptune and Pluto are furthest from the Sun in the cosmic line-up, so take longer to make one revolution, and stay longer in one sign or in aspect to another planet. This means more time for its impact to be expressed, and mould you into shape! These planets are high voltage and demand nothing but complete surrender – resistance is futile! They're cosmic markers reflecting your inner evolutionary cycle; read the signs and participate in your destiny.

You're born into a generational group sharing the same stamp of an outer planet in a particular sign. These are generational markers, the longest being Pluto, with subgroups Neptune and Uranus. The sign these planets occupy in a birth chart explains generational stamps. In transits, their archetypal meaning expresses in the outer world, flavoured by the sign hosting it, through social changes, design and technology.

This is the astro-powered heart of prediction and forecasting. Get to know their archetypal meanings, look back in history to plot how they express. Put together your own timeline so you can plot your journey so far. It's easier to understand how they may unfold in your future as they change sign, house and aspect to your natal planets. You are energy in motion, surf the cycles of development and live by your inner compass – life is precious, take your shot!

Astro Power

Uranus

⛢ Uranus

Lux et libertus · Light and liberty

Keywords · Awakens · Liberation · Revolution · Excites · Disrupts · Reform · Change · Advanced technology · Invention · Shock of the new · Progressive · Independent · Radical · Avant garde · Unconventional · Alien · Independent freedom · Revelation · High energy · Peculiar · Controversial · Reorienting

Orbit · 84 years

In a sign · 7 years

Rules · Aquarius

Functions well · Aquarius

Take special care · Leo

Function · The role of Uranus is to awaken, usually through disruption if it must. The table is turned, everything orderly is suddenly flying through the air, crashing to the floor. Next in the cosmic line up after Saturn, Uranus contrasts by shaking up established ideas, roles and institutions. It's time for change so that we progress.

Too much Saturn becomes stale, old, depleted of life and energy. It crystallizes and resists change so Uranus is the lightning bolt of liberation. Shocking, new, like a bolt out of the blue it's so progressive it seems alien. Jupiter may expand but Uranus is a quantum shift. As a higher octave of Mercury, its role is to blow your mind. This is the sudden genius revelation, ideas that get you thrown into the stocks. Ultimately its role is to liberate and achieve freedom through independence.

Uranus – the planet

The discovery of Uranus in 1781 blew the roof off the scientific establishment as the first new planet in modern history. It opened minds to the idea that there could be more if we only explored and experimented. Daring to be different, this cool blue-green ice giant spins sideways and east to west.

Uranus – the deity

Uranus is the Romanized Greek Ouranos, a personification of the sky, that faded into the background as the new generation moved into Olympus. However, the mythology of Prometheus is a better fit for the astrological meaning of Uranus.

If Mercury is the trickster, Prometheus (meaning foresight) is the supreme trickster, working on a bigger scale altogether. The most common version of the story sees Prometheus tasked with creating men from clay and giving them fire, stolen from Olympus. Furious that Prometheus had shared fire with men, Zeus ordered Hephaestus to create a beautiful woman – Pandora (the giver of gifts) – who was sent to Prometheus carrying a jar that she was told not to open. Needless to say, it was opened and all the calamities of the world were released, leaving only hope at the bottom of the jar.

As punishment, Zeus has Prometheus chained to a rock to live out their days in pain. Humans now have fire, but they also have every conceivable manner of pain and suffering released from the jar.

In a similar vein, re-interpreted into the Christian creation myth of Eve and Adam, partaking of the fruit of the tree of knowledge ends in being cast out of Eden. Humankind may pay a price for their new consciousness.

Both stories suggest the divine spark of radical knowledge or consciousness disrupting life. The messenger tends to pay a high price for delivering it. This fits the astrological Uranus, as in life when you disrupt established ideas with that brilliant new knowledge, there is fierce resistance. Galileo was tried at the inquisition for suggesting the Sun is the centre of the universe, forced to denounce it and lived out the rest of his life under house arrest. It was barely a new idea even then but took centuries to become established. Uranus follows Saturn in the planetary line-up and its role is to shake up Saturn and keep shaking until the new truth prevails over old-world views.

Uranus – the archetype

In classic Uranian 'I did it my way' approach, William Herschel was a professional musician by day and avid astronomer by night. He worked alongside his sister, Caroline Herschel, and instead of plotting stars like everyone else they catalogued and collected. On discovering Uranus, they were instantly shot to fame in a life-changing pivot. Their story embodies archetypal Uranus from the get-go. Advancing technology by making their own telescopes, they were able to spot the tiny blip no one else could see, or even consider existed. In the spirit of Uranus and all things alien, it was common belief that other planets were inhabited by life forms, and William spent a solid portion of his stargazing looking for signs! The brilliant part of this story is that discovering Uranus had made the Herschels rich. They could afford to pursue their passion full time, proving that following your inner calling provides an address for destiny to find you!

Uranus in transit on a collective level

Uranus in a sign

Uranus changes sign every seven years, which is long enough for developments to form, take hold and filter down to the masses – especially today as the pace of technology is bell-curving. As an outer planet, Uranus is one of the signs of the time, indicating trends in science and technology. The sign it's in indicates areas of disruption and trends to expect, although it's tough to predict because we don't know what we don't know. Uranus is the spark of genius and invention.

As always look back to previous timeframes when Uranus was in the same sign and note the evolution on a theme.

Uranus in Aquarius · While Uranus was in Aquarius over the turn of the millennium, the internet and affordable home computers rolled out to the masses. Other outer planets were also in Aquarius, however, we know the touch of Uranus means this is going to change the landscape and our lives forever, and so it has. The information highway connected and alienated humanity at the same time. We're still grappling with the technological beast that may be more Frankenstein's monster than it first appeared.

Uranus in Aries · From 2010 through to 2019, we saw the Aries keyword 'selfie' combine with a new tech that has filtered through society. Fitness was trending, active wear was coined and women en masse stepped into both, embracing a stronger physique.

Uranus in Taurus · As Uranus moved into couch-loving Taurus (2019), active wear relaxed into lounge wear, swapping out gym for two years on the sofa (thanks to COVID-19). The planet of destabilization and tech met up with Taurus themes resulting in fin-tech (financial technology), expansion of cryptocurrency and economic instability. Agriculture and food are ruled by Taurus – lab-grown meat with a view to mass production. Taurus rules the natural world, of which we are made, suggesting science and technology, and interventions to do with our bodies and senses. Rushed new biotechnology in a redefined mRNA vaccine perhaps? Tech implants and state-controlled bio data are on the table but not implemented en masse. In the light of Uranus changing the landscape, what lasting change will come of this technology?

Uranus in Gemini · Uranus moves into Gemini 2025–2033. We know key topics like communications will be disrupted with advances in technology. Out with the iPhone in with who knows what?! Knowing this, will you be an early adopter or investor when you see it? Or hold onto the old tech until you see everyone else adopt it first? Transport and deliveries will change, the way information is distributed and even processed is anyone's guess. Twins, doubles, avatars, holograms or the meta verse anyone?

Your Uranus squad goals

You are part of a seven-year generational group sharing a penchant for disrupting established ideas, ways of doing things and even fashion. The sign your natal Uranus occupies indicates themes and areas of disruption and the freak flag you were born to fly. Where are you in that group? Early, mid or late? If early, you are on the cutting edge; don't wait to create.

Uranus in transit on a personal level

Buckle up, transits of Uranus are by nature bumpy! If you have easy aspects, it may be a smoother ride, but it will be a fast one so be ready to quantum jump into your future.

A question on the tips of everyone's lips in online newbie astrology forums is, 'does Uranus make me gay?' The short answer is NO. Nothing can 'make' you anything than what you are. Although there is no planet queerer than this one, its role is to awaken. A transit from Uranus to, say, your Venus or Sun may indeed awaken you from your sexually conforming slumber to realize maybe it's not a girl crush, maybe I'm queer, as modern feminist and social provocateur Florence Given so aptly put it. On the other hand, if you're a straight-down-the-line hetero sapiens living in a fluid world, you're going to wake up to your truth.

Uranus is high voltage, as energizing and exciting as it is shocking and destabilizing. Use the energy and cracks in the fabric of your usual routine to create something new in your life or in the world.

Uranus transiting the houses of your birth chart

The area of life housing Uranus is up for disruption and radical change, ideally resulting in more authenticity, the expression of your unique genius, autonomy and independence. You may meet a Uranian type in this area, or they may be the catalyst for change.

Perhaps it's up to you to do the rebelling and start a personal revolution. You may be a progressive or on the edge of things, but that is exactly what will work in your favour, so don't hide under Saturn's conservative bushel. The point of Uranus is to **be** the **change**, or the change will shake and shock you until you do.

How do you need to respond to what the Uranian winds of change bring?

4th House · A classic case of itchy feet, it's time to move, or you may move unexpectedly. Tech up your home or channel this energy by moving the furniture around – a lot. Unusual or unexpected family revelations could be afoot.

7th House · You meet or experience Uranus through a relationship and this is the area being shaken. You'll be approaching relationships in a unique way, progressive compared with your background or social group. If an existing relationship is disrupted, perhaps it's because you wanted more space and independence. This is your opportunity, like it or not, to explore life and partnership that way. The more you cling to a partner at this time, the more they will have to carry the Uranian energy and act the part. Better you make the call and take the lead to design something that reflects the truth of your individual union rather than fit dominant mainstream social expectations. You may meet a Uranian type who is exciting and spontaneous.

10th House · You're leading the charge for change and it looks good on you. People respond to your individuality so work your unique look, ideas and approaches in your professional life and public image. Invite stimulation, do things differently and expect the unexpected in this area of life. Career may take a new direction without warning.

Uranus transiting the natal planets of your birth chart

As an outer planet transiting a personal planet, things are about to get wild – French Revolution wild! Around the time Uranus was discovered, women selling fish in the market were a major agent of change. Prices were impossible, bread was unaffordable, so they marched on the King's summer palace at Versailles to bring him back to Paris to deal with it. In the end, chaos ensued, tables were turned and heads rolled. If an area of your life has grown too comfortable, you're ignoring necessary change. When Uranus transits a natal planet or point, this is where, when and how the lightning strikes.

How do you need to respond to the Uranian call to freedom? What will you do with the Promethean fire of knowledge that stirs you?

Conjunct Sun · When you wake up to who you really are, it is a truly enlightening and exciting time. You're embodying the Uranian archetype, almost glowing with electrical charge and Promethian light. Don't try to shut the revelation – it's time to update who you thought you were into who you are.

Opposite Venus · A relationship or person in your life is Uranian, destabilizing or non-committal. Is this because you need independence or could do with space but won't push into unknown territory? This person is most likely stimulating and attractive to you; don't try to do the relationship the same old way. They're a catalyst for change. If someone is unavailable, what is the hidden benefit to you? Again, your evolution may require you become more independent.

Trine Jupiter · This aspect super-charges growth. An opportunity may land in your lap or you make the change and take a leap of faith. The two houses that are connected by the trine benefit each other and work well together. Uranus is stimulating your gifts and you easily understand how to make them work for you. This time involves doing things differently or getting a chance to share because the world is ready for your genius – deliver. To expand your opportunities, think way outside the box and push your creative edge.

Work your Uranus

Pack lightly and be ready for anything; this is your 'I gotta be me' moment! Make like Uranus and bolt! Break free of constraint but don't throw the baby out with the bath water. Keep what works and ditch what doesn't. You don't need to upturn your entire life – or do you?

Uranus milestones – Uranus returns

With an 84-year orbit, the Uranus cycle is long enough to make it worth watching the aspects unfold. Get a sense of how the themes manifest in your life and you'll be better able to predict the type of scenarios that repeat. You'll keep getting another chance at each turn, so you'll get better at knowing what kind of freedom you really want.

Waxing sextile · Darling, you're different. A tender and awkward age at 14, as your body is rapidly and radically changing, you're becoming your own individual, rejecting your parents, discovering yourself and getting ready to set out to find your tribe and expand your territory. Here you touch base with your spark, stay curious and experimental. You're electrically charged; jump a few levels in the game of life.

Waxing square · At 21, what psychologists are calling the quarter-life crisis, is the Saturn return leading up to 30. (Technically, that means you'll live to 120, of course, but everything is relative!) Before it shifted down to 18, 21 was always the milestone age celebrated as getting 'the keys to the door', which really means access to all areas as a young adult, drinking and meeting new people. The square is a huge shift socially, a time to consciously choose your direction. This is the time to set your course by your inner prevailing winds of change not by social or parental dictats. Do you risk it all on your dreams, doing it your way or do you take the safe route? Uranus demands my way or the highway!

Waxing trine · This cosmic jump at 28 makes adjustments easier, leading into the Saturn return. Decisions or a path you took at the square ripen and you're able to see yourself stepping up or finally moving away from expectations of your parents.

Uranus opposition 39–42 · Aka the midlife crisis! A lot happens at this phase, and if you've been conforming to external standards at the cost of your own, this is a major course correction. This time is about leaving your comfort zone, taking risks, trying new things as the cosmic jump leads connect to your energy circuits and zap you into warp speed.

Don't try to hold onto your 30's style of youth, a major pitfall for this age. Bring your youthful spirit into the next phase to build on what you've already created. Look into the future with foresight. Use the bolt of energy to make the key word of Uranus, change. Put yourself in the path of excitement; be open to reinvention and enlivenment.

Waning trine · Like the opening trine, the period around 55 is a time of ease. You've adjusted to the changes in your body, and psychologically you're able to develop your understanding, create or take opportunities. You're midway through a decade of mastery, so amplify your unique gifts and share them, the more authentic the better – people are ready.

Waning square · The three-quarter life crisis at 61–63 is another time of tension that spells a corner or fork in the road. The age of retirement is approaching; it may be time to begin winding things down or making major adjustments, perhaps hitting the road on a sabbatical, selling your business, handing over the reins or otherwise creating more space for *me* time. Interests may change and you may not want to continue the run you had through your fifties. Make your life fit you rather than trying to fit into your life.

Waning sextile · Like the sextile at 14, now you are 70 but stay curious – changes are occurring as you shift into seniority, but it's an exciting time. Internal revelations are sparked, perhaps you've settled into retirement and realize life really begins at 70! Take this great chance to reinvigorate your mindset.

Uranus return · One full cycle is complete at 84. The Promethean fire of higher knowledge is yours. You're at the 'if only I knew then what I know now' age. Well, you know it now so what will you do with this spark? A new cycle begins now so re-orient in a way that fits you, stay young at heart and choose an environment that is stimulating, not stagnant. This is the age of life expectancy in the West, when perhaps you want to plug into a spiritual and inner orientation. With the full-circle insight, you may produce or release your most meaningful work and contribution to society or to yourself.

Personal challenges and pitfalls of Uranus

Watch for disruption and change for the sake of change; think it through and be a rebel *with* a cause. Uranus transits are no time to cling to safety, security or the tried and tested; be open to change. If you feel misunderstood, ejected from a comfort zone or your known universe, know that the dust will settle.

Technology is advancing, encroaching on our lives at the expense of the natural world, making it essential to mind the pitfalls represented by Uranus. We're deferring to science unquestioned, as it fills a space reserved for spirituality. Mary Shelley's *Frankenstein* is a potent reminder of the potential outcome of over-reaching ourselves. In the rush and hubris of the Uranian urge to break new ground, we may not hit the mark. Too much emphasis on Uranian separation is alienating and, like the original Ouranos, removes us from our body, the Earth. Without balance we're ungrounded, unrealistic and lost in the deep space of our intellect, just as the original Ouranos was castrated by his offspring and cut loose from the Earth to float in the heavens.

Uranus retrograde

Uranus retrogrades for five months each year, backtracking almost 4°, then moves direct about 8°, giving a total annual progress of 4°.

If Uranus is retrograding over a sensitive point like your Sun, it means it will spend extra time there, and you'll see themes repeat and evolve. If you don't know what that theme is the first or second time, you will by the third. Make the changes and embrace the gift along with the shock of the new.

Generally, over the retrograde period things may slow down so you have time to breathe, plan for when Uranus is moving direct.

Neptune

♆ Neptune

Sequitur beatitudo · Follow your bliss (Henri de Lubac)
Keywords · Oneness · Mystic · Bliss · Numinous · Dissolution · High art ·
Sensitivity · Perceptiveness · Soulful · Spirituality · Magic · Dreams ·
Escapism · Illusion · Disillusion · Disappointment · Longing · Lowered energy ·
The muses · Belief · Altered states · Sacrifice · Redemption
Orbit · 167 years
In a sign · 14 years
Rules · Pisces
Functions well · Pisces
Take special care · Virgo
Function · Associated with what we would term mystic, spiritual or cosmic
consciousness, Neptune inspires the urge to merge, dissolving barriers to
oneness. The higher octave of Venus (personal love), Neptune is transpersonal
or impersonal love, the heart that opens in empathy to all creation and sees
themself in others and others in themself. Ultimately its goal is for you to realize
we're all connected and an emanation of the same universal intelligence. It
connects us back to our inner/higher self through dissolution, and therefore
may manifest in an expression of loss or bliss. Accessed through vehicles like
art, music, service, meditation, Neptune's world is foggy, holographic and
sometimes illusory. It's the soul factor and enchantment in our lives.

Neptune – the planet

Ruling magic and glamour, this second ice giant may rain diamonds,
like eccentric Uranus. Both planets are out of this world and are
similarly worlds away.

Neptune was discovered in 1846 on the cusp of a new movement,
spiritualism. Where science and rationalism skipped out on this
essential topic, spiritualism stepped in. The Fox sisters are credited
with sending seances viral a month after Neptune moved into its
ruling sign of Pisces. At that time mortality was high and death was
no stranger. People had a good reason to explore the metaphysical
side and it went mainstream. All things mystical are hot topics as
Neptune makes its way through Pisces once more.

Neptune – the deity

Because Neptune blurs and dissolves boundaries, it's associated with mediumship, clairvoyance and anything involving heightened sensitivity. Its extra sensory perception is delicate and rarefied.

Ancient Greco-Rome may have been all about masculine brawn and big biceps, but they weren't threatened by the mystical. One of the top jobs – and one of few careers that were open to women – was working as a professional mystic. The Pythia in Greece and Sybil in Rome were official oracles.

The Greco-Roman temple dedicated to Apollo in Delphi is built on the remains of a goddess-based predecessor, as Christian churches have been built on foundations previously occupied by Greco-Roman temples.

The Pythia channelled prophecies and answered seekers' questions. The Pythias chair was positioned above a fissure in the rock that emitted some sort of gas. Neptune rules gas, drugs and intoxication as well as channelling, mediumship and prophecy.

Neptune – the archetype

Classic archetypes include the healer, mystic, psychic, medium, artist, visionary, the addict and bleeding heart.

The Ancient worlds had plenty of outlets for the mystical archetype of Neptune to express. Everything was seen to have a spirit with a deity embodying it. Today we have the same desire to contact the divine through direct experience, which has seen Neptune come to the fore: people en masse seeking altered states of consciousness, meditation going mainstream and crystals galore. Astrology and tarot are frameworks to tap into our higher mind. While seances haven't been trending as hard as they did around Neptune's discovery, slipping back through time to connect with ancestors, the rise of the modern mystic and dissolving of boundaries from identity to sexuality are manifestations. More people are discovering their creative side, inviting in Neptune.

From 40000–4000BC, 90% of figurines represented women as the archetypal divine source of life, dropping dramatically to 0.5%; an excellent reason to reclaim the divine. Women and alternative voices, silenced through much of history, are repopulating digital platforms.

In various tribal cultures, non-gender-conforming people were believed to possess heightened access to spirituality and a little more magic than regular folk – hallmarks of Neptune – as they had two spirits. Today's two-spirits are queer, gay, fluid, non-binary and trans people, enriching our world.

Neptune in transit on a collective level

When we look back and remember a particular decade, it's Neptune's markers we recognize in the spirit of the times. Trends in fashion, themes in film, colours, spirituality and even forms of escapism are indicated by the sign hosting Neptune. Since Neptune is expressed through the arts, it's possible to cast into the future and make predictions about what will be hot and what will not.

Neptune in a sign

Neptune in Scorpio · Mid-1955–1970 · Sacred sexuality · The pill liberated women and the sexual revolution was on. Taboos were dissolved over this period. Elvis shocked in 1956 with his racy moves, earning him the name Elvis the Pelvis; waistlines dropped, emphasizing the pelvic area that is ruled by Scorpio; and who can forget the music festival of Woodstock?

The counterculture abandoned the expectations and pressures of the 1950s. They tuned in through psychedelics, exploring the psychological, and dropped out of the materialist pursuits of capitalism. Films explored confronting, psychological themes with X-rated *Midnight Cowboy* winning three Academy Awards.

Scorpio is a sign prepared to provoke, ready to sting if it must. Waking up to some hard social realities, people protested a variety of essential civil rights.

Sagittarius · 1970–1984 · Soul seekers · Sagittarius rules travel and the search for higher meaning, so it's a great fit for Neptune. Travellers went to India and bought Eastern spirituality back to the West as Tibetan monk Chogyam Trungpa moved to the US and began teaching. An ethnic look came into fashion and proportion was exaggerated with bell bottoms, big glasses and big hair. The blockbuster was born and shows co-starred or headlined animals like Benji, a scruffy heroic little dog, Grizzly Adams and BJ and the Bear. Greenpeace and PETA were founded as Sagittarius is connected to the natural world. *Star Wars* summed up the combination of humour, spirituality and adventure.

Pisces · 2011–2025 · Modern mystics · When in Pisces, Neptune in its own rulership is at maximum expression. The mystic went mainstream, arts and spirituality exploded through social media, a dissolving influence on identity and sexuality as well as boundaries between social divisions ensued. Cross-species empathy expressed as a bell curve in vegan diet choice with new dining options catering to growing demand. This period will surely be remembered for the dominance of rainbows and unicorns, two symbols synonymous with Neptune and Pisces. The soft millennial pink wash is dominating colour schemes, while astrology, crystals, tarot and oracles are trending. There's something fishy going on; 'Instagram face' is pushing the illusory beauty ideal into impossible territory while invasive procedures and digital filters are enhancing the 'fish pout' and expressionless upper face. Streaming platforms made their own content and we binged ourselves into fantasy.

Neptune in Aries 2025–to 2038 · Spiritual warriors · Neptune in Aries begins a new cycle in the first sign of the zodiac and heralds a markedly different tone to the Pisces era. The sign of the times will change from soft millennial pinks to reds, bright energetic colour and design. This is a super yang sign so it may externalize through physicality. Martial arts, Tai Chi, or even transcending through challenging your body and mind like walking on coals or spirit quests in the wild may become more popular.

Spirituality combines with a self-oriented approach to bliss. Trends in fashion, art and film may be bold and robust, emphasizing strength and the hero. The last time Neptune was in Aries, people fought the good fight in the American civil war, sacrificing themselves for the agency and independence of others.

Your Neptune squad goals

Your Neptune squad is the 14-year age bracket you share the spiritual pool with. The way you approach, consume and create art, fashion, design and spirituality will have a strong stamp of the sign Neptune was in when you were born. Millennials have Neptune in Capricorn, so have dissolved the boundary between the mystic and business with spiritually focused business and the mystical component as the product. Beautiful co-working spaces brought people together, and the girl boss rebranded professional life. With Neptune in Aquarius, Gen Z are the true millennials, accessing spirituality through technology, groups and networks. Perhaps they'll do for the internet what millennials did for business. Be aware of your group's approach and see how you can contribute, partake authentically or cater to a specific group.

Neptune in transit on a personal level

Neptune transiting the houses of your birth chart

Neptune will be in this area of your life for quite some time, so it's worth checking in to see how it's unfolding. Look back at the previous house, or two if you're old enough to have had it travel three zones. Since Neptune is seeking dissolution, this zone is a temple over the period of the transit. Knowing where you're hosting Neptune will keep you mindful of its expressions, so you avoid pitfalls and make the most of it. Boundaries may be questionable;

people may not be what they seem because you're idealizing them and you're more permeable. But this is where you meet Neptune. Experience mystical moments that part the veil. You have Neptune on your side, so use the power of glamour wisely.

7th House · Here you meet, look for and express Neptune through the house of the other person, perhaps by meditating together or collaborating artistically. Watch for idealizing someone or setting an ideal or fantasy they can't live up to – you'll only be disappointed. Be certain the Neptunian types you meet – sensitive, perhaps artistic – are truly spiritual, not escaping through addiction. You're a psychic sponge with a soft spot for the vulnerable, so maintain healthy boundaries as you open up to a beautiful spiritual union.

10th House · Meet the mystical through your career. You may be idealistic about outcomes, so avoid disappointment by pegging your efforts to a higher cause and invite the muses to work through you. Intention is everything and magic can happen. A creative element, ability to connect or soulfully create is essential. Arts careers are an easy A with Neptune.

11th House · Spiritual friendships or a common artistic interest will keep Neptune happy. Lose yourself in the crowd at festivals and big events or hang out with an ashram or yoga community. Perhaps lead spiritual workshops, a meditation group or get involved with a charitable service. Your friendships may dissolve if they're not inline, so let them go for this period. The space Neptune makes is for a reason.

Neptune transiting the natal planets of your birth chart

Neptune is an outer planet, beguilingly powerful in its slow wash cycle of your life. It opens and makes porous anything it touches. Avoid intoxicants, toxins and dishonest people. Take up a simple spiritual practice or an easy everyday ritual and cleanse your energy and space regularly, with intention.

Neptune conjunct Sun · Neptune dissolves solar themes: the ego, identity, sense of self. Open to more than you thought you were, expect a spiritual tone or softening of your identity. You may feel lost, extra sensitive and vitality/energy may decrease. The point is to call you into yourself; it's super-yin. Take the spiritual road. Eat organic or as cleanly as possible to avoid toxins.

This is a glamorous transit and one that can plug you into the collective thirst for transcendence. Due to the mystique of Neptune, you easily resonate with the times because you reflect them simply by being yourself.

Neptune square Mercury · The square represents challenge to your way of thinking, understanding, listening, communication and interests. What is causing tension? Is it an external or an internal requirement for change? It may be time to reorient your interests, understand the symbolic and let go of a mechanistic mindset. This suggests direct experience; trusting your inner voice and perception isn't easy, but it's time to move your perception to the next level. You may feel your words are misunderstood or language can't encapsulate meaning. In that case, turn to poetry, visual imagery or perhaps symbolic oracles like tarot. If you are the confused one, double-check important data or facts. Your intuition may be perceptive but you lose track of time and your ability to focus; pin down detail and deadlines. Watch for deception and illusion and run plans by a sensible friend. Great for visions and working both creatively and intuitively.

Work your Neptune

Tune in, enchant your world. Meditate, slow down and sense your environment, let it light you up. Listen to your inner voice, journal your dreams and foster a connection through them to your subconscious. Practise tarot or consult oracles. Listen to the first thought and notice when your rational mind comes in with the 'logic'. Practise astrology as a framework and invite your inner voice to speak. Chant with friends or invest in a sound bowl. Do a course that facilitates your psychic awareness. Develop an art form like music, dance or painting to balance out your day-to-day intellectual life. Get in touch with your magic, create from the infinite void through manifesting. Experiment with ritual, vision boarding and future timelining. Intention is everything. Then bring in the Neptune and start the ball rolling with practical steps.

Neptune milestones

Neptune is slow so you'll never have a Neptune return. Neptune's generic cycle represents your spiritual or artistic development, your relationship with your inner divine wellspring and development of selfless compassion.

Sextile · At 28, around the same time as your Saturn return, the ease of the sextile helps you find your connection to your inner voice, perhaps your spirituality or the vehicle you choose to connect with it. A good time for ease in manifesting, which helps oil the wheels of change as you enter the next Saturn cycle. Listen to your inner calling so you move in a direction of destiny, not external expectation.

Neptune square · This aspect is the main headline of the Neptune cycle, and a midlife crisis marker at 41. In this case it may be a spiritual crisis as you realize you're not fulfilled in an area of your life. Make a change to accommodate your spiritual needs.

Trine · The mid-fifties are cruise mode with a number of flowing aspects. You're at ease with your spirituality and this is a time of manifesting.

Opposition · The opposition at 82 reflects a time of harvest and blossoming, from this point it's time to turn in. You may devote more time to your spirituality, experience a catalyst to do so or spend time with a person who is a Neptunian type.

Personal challenges and pitfalls of Neptune

Okay, it looks like there's a lot of pitfalls – from disappointment and delusion to addiction and lethargy – but they balance the gifts of Neptune. Like anything, Neptune is a coin with two sides. In the end it's an authentic connection with spirit vs inauthentic. Only you know, as it's a direct experience. You can't buy, emulate, get it from or through someone else. If you're escaping through addiction to food, screens, drugs, sex or anything else, tap into an authentic spirit so you have a connection to the divine.

Culturally the biggest pitfalls are people who build a paywall around the well, so to speak: religions or cult leaders who promise they can facilitate salvation, or rationalists who depend on science to provide what only soul can.

The god /saviour complex

When the ego unravels too quickly or gets bloated and mistaken for spiritual connection you quickly become ungrounded. Losing touch with reality and other people isn't healthy or helpful to your journey. On the other hand, a spiritual emergency may appear as a breakdown, but it's an opportunity to let go of an identity that's inauthentic and too constricting. Be around people who facilitate your journey and care for you until you make it out the other side into your more authentic self.

The trick with Neptune is ego. Treat it like a loved child and let it know it's valued but can't take over.

Neptune retrograde

Neptune retrogrades just over five months a year, so spends extended time over one area. That's a time to pay extra attention to your inner world. Note when aspects to personal planets or points are exact and how many times the retrograde will connect, then you're better prepared for the fog.

Pluto

♇ Pluto

Magnus transfigurator · The great transformer
Keywords · Power · Death and rebirth · Transformation · Intensity ·
Regeneration · Taboo · Crisis · Dominance · Destruction · Shadow · Depth ·
Obsession · Explosive · Decay · Survival instinct · Compulsion · Will to live ·
Magnetism · Underworld
Orbit · 247 years
In a sign · 11.5–30 years
Rules · Scorpio
Take special care · In Taurus
Function · Not one for polite society, this heavy hitter's role is about power in
all its forms: the power of life and death, power to annihilate and the power to
transform and regenerate. Along with balance and use of power is the control
and sharing, or manipulation, of it.

Pluto is what we sweep under the carpet and all things taboo. It's the really
hard stuff. It's dark and thick and oily, and it coats everything.

Like an explosive volcano, Pluto's role is to purge. It's the higher octave of
Mars, so its power is total. After volcanic eruptions, life returns, often more
fecund. Don't resist this natural process. With a slow burn that builds in intensity,
note what's decaying; cut out dead or rotting wood and let it go. If something
has been buried or unresolved, exhume it to finish the process of death so it can
continue to the next cycle.

Representing the hidden, what's in the dark out of sight, Pluto outs secrets.
It's the process of lancing, purging poison and bringing it to light so it can live in
a new form. To be truly empowered, you've got to be comfortable with owning
and wielding your power. Pluto's transits give you every opportunity to do that.

Pluto – the dwarf planet

Pluto finally got it's close-up in 2015, the same year as #metoo
came out of Hollywood and into public awareness. It turns out
Pluto sports an enormous heart-shaped glacier the size of Texas
and Oklahoma. Pluto's public image has changed from creeping
in a lonely, dark corner of space, to warm and fuzzy memes ready
to be loved and included, reflective of the power of love and
support for the women who shared their stories.

Pluto – the deity

The power of death and rebirth was represented as a chthonic (Earth/underworld) aspect of the Great Goddess in many manifestations, since the ultimate power is the ability to create life, and no one can cheat death. Snakes were a venerated symbol of her Earth aspect because they lived underground. As snakes shed their skin, they don't stop at apparent death, and neither does the cycle of nature as evidenced by the annual cycle of the seasons, day and night. The symbol of the Ouroboros, the circular snake or dragon eating its own tail, illustrates the point.

For almost 2,000 years anyone who could speak Ancient Greek was welcome to take part in the Eleusinian Mysteries. The cycle of rebirth was seen in the wheat grain disappearing under the ground, only to reappear as new life. Held around harvest season in early autumn, it was a fall equinox festival symbolizing the dying Sun.

Cicero said it best: 'We have learned from the fundamental of life and have grasped the basis not only for living with joy, but also for dying with better hope.' Held at the Temple of Demeter, the myth centres around Demeter and her daughters' decent to the underworld, leaving the world barren of life and joy, then returning to life. It's thought a potent psychedelic brew, passed through the throng of up to 3,000, along with meaningful rites, tied spiritual experience to seasonal change. Facing and surviving death of the ego, beyond the illusion of the mundane world, people were freer to live and less fearful of death. Philosophers of the day like Socrates, Plato and Plutarch attended these rites, influencing culture long after their consciousness-altering experiences in the great underground hall at Eleusis.

Pluto – the archetype

Social scientist Brene Brown is the poster figure for how to do Pluto the healthy way. A Pluto-ruled Scorpio, she weighs in on the global conversation around the toxic dark side; shame, guilt, secrecy, vulnerability and how we can bring it to the light, and lead courageously. People who have been side-lined through systems of power are speaking up. Taking back power, they're diminishing the only real power of would-be abusers, secrecy.

The books *1984* and *The Lord of the Rings* were written by authors who experienced the Plutonic horrors of large-scale war first hand. A cautionary tale is evident in both works.

Around the same time that Pluto was discovered in the 1930s, nuclear power was discovered, resulting in the immense destructive power of the atomic bomb; small things can make a big impact: the small things that gnaw from the inside or the one ping that sets off inner grenades.

Society needs a healthy outlet for this archetype, which is why the Eleusinian rites were so enduring. At its most perverse with the witch-hunts, it's our own demons we need to address – the shadow part of oneself we repress as unacceptable and therefore scapegoat or deny. It's a tough archetype to handle and even talk about as it carries a powerful charge when triggered. However, the past few years it's surfaced and is being dealt with thanks to women and alternative voices to the mainstream having a forum on social media.

Pluto in transit on a collective level

Pluto rules power as well as hidden wealth, but it is back-room power. It also rules mystery, a deeply transformative process, sometimes involving purging, cutting back or annihilation as prep to start again with a clean slate. At its slowest, Pluto manages to grind forward 1° in a year. At its fastest it's still laboriously slow, at 3°, like pushing a tank through toffee, allowing plenty of time for transformation that is deep, thorough and complete.

Pluto in a sign

Industries and areas ruled by the host sign are all up for explosive bombshells and will be forever transformed by the end of the transit. Expect scandals and social transformation around sex, money, power and wealth.

Capricorn 2008 · Capricorn rules traditional, established systems and structures of power, authority and control. The government, big institutions and corporations as well as the people who run them or benefit from those systems. When Pluto comes along, this is the area up for transformation. Power is gained as well as stripped. As Pluto moved into Capricorn, the global financial crisis hit after the housing bubble burst. Capricorn is associated with the economy and limitation as well a serving as a reality check. Businesses 'too large to fail' have been described as being on 'life support'; they were bailed out – both Capricorn and Pluto themes. Capitalism is about the strong surviving with the market dictating; how long can top-down power last through Pluto's transit? One thing we know is that these areas will be completely transformed, either centralizing power and tightening control, exploding or imploding. Business was transformed over this period as more people were able to start up online with no bricks-and-mortar shopfront and next to no investment.

Aquarius 2024 · Transformation, power and control of and through technology, society, information and science are featured here. Humanitarian and social issues may undergo deep change. Power to the people or over the people? Our views on the reality of our universe may transform through an emphasis on science and rationalism. While we potentially get the enlightening side of Aquarius' brilliance of intellectual rigour and invention, we may also see the dark side of technology. Will that be through control of information, centralizing citizen data or decentralizing power?

Open source and collective information, powerful crowd sourcing and social evolution, robots, aliens – will they figure? What new discovery will rock us to our core?

Pluto squad goals

The generational markers used by society like 'Generation X' and 'millennials' correlate with the sign Pluto occupies in the birth chart. These groupings break down further into sub-groups and will share one of two Neptune signs, and the two to three possible signs Uranus will be found in. These planets retrograde back and forth over the cusps, so check your birth chart for accuracy and draw up your diagram to see how the outer planets fit into your astro-coding.

The sign you share with your Pluto generation is the area of transformation that affected your squad as you came into the world, and what you're here to reveal, purge and transform. It may show the kind of power struggles and imbalance you face through your life.

1971–1984 · 2nd group of Gen X · Pluto in Libra · This period sees transformation around equality, justice, fairness and partnerships; will to power through design, the arts and beauty; powerful peacekeepers and collaborators. This generation was born as civil rights activists demanding equality, equal pay, representation and respect. Protesting hit peak intensity as people gathered in consciousness-raising groups. More women had access to work, so this was the first group to see women enter the public sphere in bigger numbers. They presided over marriage equality, demanded beauty and redesigned everyday objects from utilitarian to beautiful. They may be quiet achievers and the peacemaker between the Boomer vs Millennial beef (their Pluto signs square each other) but Generation X, as an Air sign, has higher education, controls more wealth per capita, killing it with start-ups, and as a Venus-ruled cardinal sign quietly influencing the influencers.

1983–1995 · Millennials · Pluto in Scorpio · Millennial astrologer Kirah Tabourn says her generation had access to the internet before cyber child locks were in place. Too much adult sexual content too young, these self-proclaimed swamp creatures are here to plunge and purge sexual taboos and reclaim their primal and sacred sexuality. Dating apps transformed how people connect, providing the privacy Scorpio cleaves to. Mating and dating without leaving the bedroom! This group brought us emo, awareness of difficult feelings, trauma awareness and the anonymous hoodie.

1995–2008 · Gen Z · Pluto in Sagittarius · The first to grow up with the internet, Gen Z is already globally connected, which means a naturally broad-ranging awareness of global issues and possibilities. Born at a time when terrorism transformed international travel, and educational institutions were booming and busting, younger Gen Z has faced completing school or college online. Thanks to COVID lockdowns, they've moved further into online social spaces, broadening networks with no boundaries. This is a highly adaptable Fire sign that's big on communication so they won't go unnoticed. It's going to get loud and they'll tell it like it is. Expect to learn through dark humour, memes and clever video bites.

Pluto in transit on a personal level

Pluto is tough but with a lot of talk about power, this is where the rubber hits the road. You can't power drill without holding the drill. You have to wield it, stand strong in it. Transits from Pluto unlock deep reservoirs of energy, resources you never knew you had, and open your awareness to a deeper side of life.

Pluto transiting the houses of your birth chart

This area of life is where you will meet, experience and express Plutonic themes. There may be power struggles, a dominating person, obsession that puts you in the ring, face to face with what you hold shame or fear around and have generally buried in your psychic basement. Look to your dreams for clues and listen to your intel. Pluto transits can be like a laser-sharp X-ray into other people's basements as like can see like. In the vein of the great goddess and cycle of life, Brene Brown says it's never too late to circle back. Revisit the part of yourself that you may have hidden, secrets you feel but don't know the details about or conflicts that seem to boil out of nowhere. You'll come out of this transit unshakable, so go in ready for a s/heroic decent into the underworld and fly out as the phoenix, unburdened, aflame and free.

Ascendant/1st House · This transit is world-changing, as your outlook undergoes deep structural change. It may coincide with a challenging situation that reorients, or like Frodo in *The Lord of the Rings*, sets you on your quest for empire, power and wealth. Let go of what you need to and build something better.

4th House · Invest in someone to help you do up your home or your own emotional underpinnings. Look at all the stuff that isn't seen: rotting foundations or stagnant emotions. Therapy at this time is a way to go with the Plutonic penchant for plumbing the depths. If there are power struggles or skeletons under the floorboards, you'll find them during this period.

6th House · Work may be the primary source of conflict, power struggle or intensity. You may need to transform through your work or leave and find work that gives you the sort of challenge and satisfaction you crave. Step into your power and make a deep impact. Take care of your health and focus on cleaning out toxins, this a good time for a deep cleanse and total overhaul of your fitness and health routine. Power and transformation are through daily routine and habit.

Pluto transiting the natal planets in your birth chart

All your shadow work is ready to roll out, witches! If you have a handle on Plutonian themes, you may savour the deepening that accompanies Pluto. A crevice in your soul and psyche opens and in you go to discover your underworld. This is your primal engine room, the seat of the survival instinct. It's primitive and purposeful when you know how to drive it!

Pluto conjunct Mercury · Your interest may turn to major intellectual challenges such as psychology, metaphysics, big research or a writing project. Give your mind a worthy goal and something to chew on as this placement can signal obsessive thinking. If your mind locks onto something that you can't shake, you'll need to dig down to what's beneath it. Talk therapy is a guided tour of your psyche and will prove fascinating. Your power of insight is potent, keep an open and curious, non-judgemental approach to what you see in yourself and others. Dreams may feature volcanic or burnt-out dark landscapes, birth, death or other Plutonic themes; keep a journal and reflect on them. Explore the power of your mind and the transformational power of thought.

Pluto square Moon · This is a painful and slow transit. Pluto creates tension to your sense of emotional security, fear around your mother, death, nurturing and primal survival instinct. If you have trauma from birth, this is your chance to explore, purge and transform it. All the darkest themes like betrayal, jealousy and obsession come to light. Keep an eye on what comes up for you so it doesn't take you over. It will pass, so make necessary changes and let go.

Pluto trine Sun · Sexy and dangerous, Pluto's easy flow to your Sun suggests heightened personal power and intensity. You're magnetic and feel like you could conquer the world. Set yourself a worthy project or goal. Renewal of your sense of self, ego, vitality and the way you express yourself are all supporting positive self-development. Who you are is changing, so go with it.

Work your Pluto

Do shadow work, see a good psychologist, explore your fears with the intention of enlightenment. Address your relationship with power or power dynamics and own your power. This is the atomic energy of destiny calling. Don't repress it, swim in it like Kali, embody it, experiment, role play and feel it.

Pluto milestones

Pluto square · Pluto's slow surge through the zodiac means there is only one major milestone aspect, the square. Due to the elliptical orbit, that could occur anywhere between 35 and 91, so your generation will face the challenges of handling power once this occurs. A power struggle may happen, or decay in an area of your life that creates tension as you hold onto what is burning. Let it go and plant the seeds of tomorrow in its ashes.

Personal challenges and pitfalls of Pluto

In the mid 1800s, writer John Dalberg-Acton said 'Power corrupts, great power corrupts completely' followed by 'Great men are almost always bad'; these sum up the will to power of Pluto. When power has no limit that's the pitfall of Pluto.

Pluto is the darkest and most difficult planet with the biggest payload if you're willing to make the journey and face your shadow, fear of mortality and true power. Stare down social controls of shame and guilt and work your way through the landscape. Watch for projecting your shadow, your greatest fears, onto someone else, scapegoating is all Plutonian shadow. That could also be around sex, sexuality, morality, power, influence, money and anything you have a difficult relationship with. Work towards liberating your vital force rather than using it to suppress parts of yourself.

Pluto retrograde

Pluto is slow-moving and retrogrades for five to six months per year, so it may not make a perceptible difference. However, if you're sensitive to this archetype, note the time it changes and the duality of the part of the year it is directly against when it retrogrades.

Pluto generations and sub-generations

Find the combination of signs the outer planets were in when you were born.

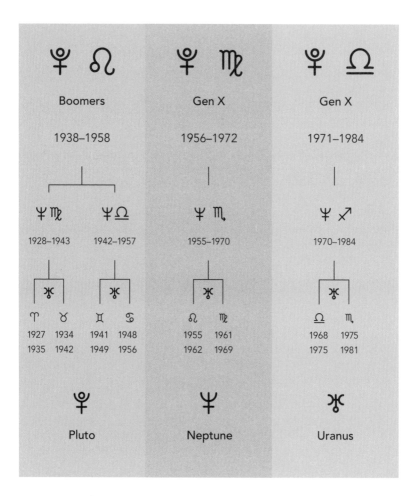

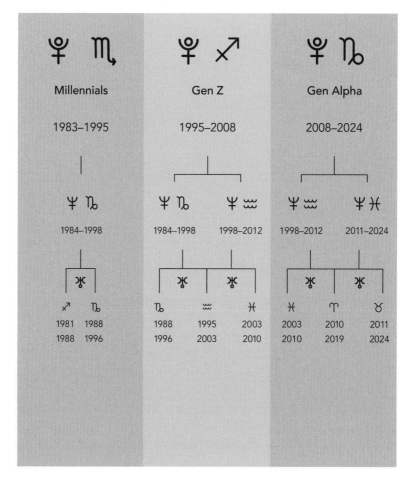

The north and south lunar nodes

The north and south lunar nodes

Fatum amplectere · Embrace destiny

Orbit · 18.6 years

In a sign · 18.6 months

Annual progress · 1° per 18.6 days so 19–20° per year

Function · Dial into your destiny with the north and south nodes, aka the dragon's head and the dragon's tail.

The north node is your North Star; it represents the direction you need to strive towards. Sounds great but this is unfamiliar, as yet undeveloped territory (according to the sign and house it's in). Because it's new you may avoid it or not even know how to 'do' your north node, so it takes a leap of faith and belief in your calling.

The south node represents your past – the part of the self that is overdeveloped, perhaps over your younger years, through your family, over lifetimes, or one particular lifetime you've incarnated from in this life. Regardless of what your beliefs are around past lives, reincarnation or karma, it's the same outcome. You start off with a natural comfort zone and resources signified by the south node and must develop the area signified by the north node placement.

The rule of thumb is that by activating the north node, things work out. If you hang out in your comfort zone, you experience the shadow side, causing discomfort, which should encourage you to leave its lair and use the gifts you have in service of your destiny.

Visit the south node leisure lounge, like a weekender, and house party your heart out. But go back to work in your own little cabin and get on with things at the north node. It may not be as glamorous as that expensive Airbnb you rented, but it's the place you'll create your destiny from and where you need to be to meet that destiny – it gives back more than you put in. The dragon only flies one direction, so don't be downwind too long or you'll end up with more than egg on your face.

The lunar nodes

When astrologers say 'nodes', or 'the north and south nodes', we're referring to the lunar nodes, or nodes of the Moon. Technically, they're the point where the Moon crosses the line of the ecliptic, which is the path the Sun travels around the Earth.

The nodes are exactly opposite each other. They move backwards through the zodiac and if you draw their path as they retrograde, they form a wavy, serpentine line. After moving (backwards) for four months, they slow or stall for two to three months, then back to four, and the cycle repeats. These are called the true nodes. However, the average calculation (mean node) is also used, so be aware of which one you're using. The true node is better for precision prediction.

There are multiple eclipse cycles called Saros cycles. If drawn, each one looks like a snake curling its way, one eclipse at a time, around the world from the south Pole to the north, or vice versa. If you had a particularly dramatic eclipse experience, check back along that Saros cycle. Each eclipse is related at 18-year increments.

Archetypal lunar nodes

Indian Vedic mythology of the nodes involves the dragon's head called Rahu, and tail, called Ketu. The dragon is spliced in the middle, separating both ends. In Western history, the nodes are also represented as a dragon, but not spliced. Rahu is always hungry for experience, gobbling it up but not able to hold onto it, to ingest or integrate it. It swallows the Sun, but the Sun slips out through the splice in Rahu, or must be regurgitated by Ketu, the tail.

Eclipse cycle

The nodes are tightly configured with themes of the Sun and Moon. Wherever you find the nodes marks where eclipses will form, so when the nodes are in Aries and Libra, these are the signs hosting eclipses for that 18-month period.

At least two solar eclipses occur annually, one at the south node and one at the north. Since the Sun, Moon and Earth must be in alignment for an eclipse to occur, eclipses are solar and lunar in nature, suggesting we manifest them here on Earth as our destiny. The north node has a solar quality. It suggests making something conscious, bringing it to the light as part of our self-development. It indicates the path we must strive for – our destiny.

The south node is considered lunar consciousness. Since the Moon is reflective, associated with the past, memory and unconscious impressions, it suggests we alchemize these through the north node's light of consciousness, through pursuing our destiny. Align your heart and head, just as the planets are aligned.

Lunar eclipses occur at Full Moon, solar eclipses are at New Moon. On a Full Moon eclipse, the Earth is aligned between the Sun and Moon, the lunar nature is reset with dominance going to the solar aspect. What emotional issues and lunar associations come to light over this period: home, security, food, nurture.

On a New Moon, the Moon is aligned between the Sun and Earth, eclipsing the Sun. The solar principle is eclipsed and reset. What is revealed is around ego, identity, self-expression.

When eclipses occur on a sensitive point or planet, it may be like a vortex or worm hole opening or slamming shut. Seen as a powerful omen, in the past there was a lot of fear and trepidation around eclipses because they were so dramatic. To reorient towards your destiny, there has to be change.

The lunar nodes transit on a collective level

The signs hosting the nodes suggest a collective theme repeating every 18.6 years. Look back at what happened previously to get a reference point for the current cycle. The sign hosting the south node may suggest themes describing what is subordinated, repressed or inactive. This may be to direct us to themes associated with the sign hosting the north node. In terms of the Vedic perspective, the north node devours experience, moving onto the next immediately, always wanting more.

Gemini north node · Sagittarius south node · The north node may not have a moral expression, but simply point to themes of major events for that period of time. The last time the south node was in Sagittarius was during the COVID-19 pandemic in 2020–2022.

Gemini and Sagittarius form the travel, education and communication axis and we experienced serious disharmony through vastly differing narratives, misinformation, conspiracy theories (Gemini) and an inability to express the truth (Sagittarius south node).

Over this period, we heard direct personal experiences and perspectives around cultural issues, and new small independent news providers and commentators gained traction. We learned a lot about language use, pronouns, insights from ethnic minority groups on topics like colourism, and perspectives along the lines of privilege. People read more books, with all the extra house-bound time, and digital communication stocks like Zoom, soared.

Saturn occupied Aquarius at the time, adding its focus on humanitarian issues, activism and education. Gemini is an Air sign, ruling the lungs, breath and hands. Covid was airborne, impacted the lungs, and hands were emphasized through sanitation.

It may have been beyond our scope to predict exactly how this period would unfold, but we knew the themes and window of time, which means we knew when the focus would shift.

The lunar nodes transit on a personal level

The lunar nodes in a house of your birth chart

As the north node travels back through your chart, the house it occupies is a focal point for that period. Utilize the resources of the house the south node is travelling through, but don't get caught up in affairs of that area. Visualize the dragon with its head in the direction you need to be focusing on, don't hang about at its tail.

1st House NN · In the 1st House, your destiny is built on your direction and outlook. The south node in your 7th House of relationships suggests this isn't the area you're meant to be focusing on. Eclipses on the ascendant/descendant are powerful. In the 7th House you may feel the impact through a partner's experience, indirectly direct. A partnership could drop out if it's not the right one for you, or suddenly appear. An eclipse in the 1st House could see you adjusting your direction, look, sense of self or experience a physical change that reorients you, depending on the sign it's in.

2nd House NN · If the north node is travelling through your 2nd House of money and resources, don't get caught up in the south node's emotional dramas of the 8th House. Stabilize your own resources. Utilize and build your personal resources, not someone else's. Although you may call on contacts or accept an investor there's one way it's meant to head: into your bank account.

4th House NN · The nodal axis is across your domestic and professional house axis. You may have your career sorted but it relies on your foundation to support it. Your home and domestic scene are the focus of this period, make sure it's the right fit. This house axis will be where the eclipses occur, so one or the other may change drastically to push you through a one-way door in the direction that will best serve you. You may learn more about the people you share your home with, or your own emotional underpinnings. This could be a good time to find a home or family house that will meet your needs over this next cycle. Set yourself up as you might be spending valuable time here.

The lunar nodes aspecting a personal planet in your birth chart

The north node destiny point passing over a natal planet indicates it's time to activate that planet. It may reveal the type of person that crosses your path (that expresses the archetype of that planet), beneficial at that time, or the nature of a catalyst for change.

The south node over the same point would suggest this is not the direction to move in or focus on, however the wealth it represents could be used to push your needle forward in the direction of the north node.

Transiting north node opposite natal Venus · A relationship isn't the direction to move in, but you may draw inspiration from a past relationship. Someone may come back into your life but it's the tail end – don't get back into the relationship, move forward independently. If you're concerned, use the north node as the antidote and move towards independence according to the sign and house it's occupying.

Transiting north node conjunct natal Sun · This suggests a solar person, someone well known, confident or a leader type is part of your destiny. Or it could mean you are meant to lead, to shine, to be yourself rather than represent someone else. It may be a time of self-understanding and self-development in service towards your destiny, which happens to play a part in your recognition in the area/house of your natal Sun. This is not a time to be a wallflower or self-depreciating, it's a time to shine, express yourself!

Transiting Venus conjunct natal north node · When a planet transits your natal north node it activates your destiny according to the planet doing the activation. Venus crossing your north node suggests a partnership, relationship, pleasant experience or person, or benefit via a Venusian person. Work your Venus!

The bending

When a transiting planet forms a square to your nodes it's at the bending. It means this planet is at maximum tension yet is integral to meeting your destiny. It needs to be integrated so may be the squeaky wheel requiring attention. Mars in square may mean you need to activate the Mars principle, get active, lead in the house that Mars is moving through rather than act against your destiny or in spite of it. If you do, you may influence, meet or otherwise take an action that's in line with your destiny, or comes around later in the cycle.

Lunar node milestones

Your nodal return occurs every 18.6 years so your first is at 18–19, then again at ages 37, 56 and 75. Halfway through the cycle is your nodal opposition. Track the points of the cycle to get an idea of how it's unfolding in your life. Since the south node is like buried treasure, when the opposition occurs, it's time to dig! Focus on your natural abilities and keep an eye out for familiar or karmic connections. This is a balance point where you'll have more idea about your destiny, regroup and refocus your efforts and direction.

Work your lunar nodes

Most of the language around the nodes is about battling your past or lower self, symbolized as the solar slaying the lunar, the hero slaying the dragon. However, the thing you're battling is yourself – or your lower nature rather than the higher expression. Rather than generate internal conflict why not shift perspective from domination to listening to and working with your lunar and solar nature.

The lunar subconscious awareness is your body's intelligence, which includes your stored memory, cellular memory, DNA, epigenetics and intel your subconscious picks up. It makes sense to create a dialogue so they work together as rudders.

Tap into the meaning of your nodes by dialoguing with your inner self. Set the intention that you want to know more about this aspect of yourself; your past life gifts and pitfalls, and your destiny. Set your intention on learning more about your lunar south node past life. Ask why it's a comfort zone, and what the lesson is you're here to figure out to direct towards your north node, what that direction looks and feels like. This will get you in touch with that precious part of yourself that knows all but speaks a language of symbol, myth, story, feeling and sensation. Learn the way this part of you communicates, trust it and you'll navigate to your destiny in flow with the cosmos.

V.

Putting it all together

If you have followed my advice, you will have been working out a short interpretation at a time and gradually building on your knowledge. Now this is where all the moving parts come together.

A birth chart is technically the same as a transit chart, also called a horoscope. They're both a snapshot of the sky at a precise moment in time, as seen from a specific location on Earth.

However, what we are doing here is reading and applying them a little differently to broaden the scope of your knowledge and its application to your life. Any single interpretation will be a sliver of potential expressions, each one chosen and laid over the last. But remember that this isn't a cookbook of every possible combination because I want you to learn to combine the meanings for yourself rather than rely on someone else's interpretation. You are the best person to assess your life; reach through the astrological framework and combine the oracular meaning revealed from within.

Technical support

Most of you will be using apps to create and view your horoscope charts and they will all have slightly different features. However, I keep my astrology simple as there's so much already going on and I find it is usually best to stick to the basics in this book to start with, then branch out when you begin to grow in confidence.

For example, some apps overlay up to three charts in a tri-wheel. Some may have options for selecting more points to feature in the chart, like asteroids and Arabic parts, also known as *lots* (from traditional astrology), so if something unique calls you, incorporate it into your method or try it out once you've mastered the fundamentals.

House system and zodiac choice

As mentioned in the section on aspects, choose the Placidus house system. It's the most widely used in modern astrology and the system used in this book. Choose the tropical zodiac. Some apps – like AstroGold – only use this system, whereas others may have several options, so check the default.

Aspect grid

Some apps feature an aspect grid like the ones I've included in this book (overleaf). You can see the connections between planets more easily by referencing this grid. Many apps feature a written list of planetary aspects, signs and placements, which is especially useful for beginners. In this case, check the aspect grid if you're unsure of how to read the aspects straight off the horoscope wheel.

Since we are using the five major aspects, be aware most apps will list extra aspects called minor aspects. Some astrologers don't use them at all and some do. Start with the top five I've listed in this book, then note others once you're confident. Personally, if a semi-square is within one degree or exact from an outer planet to an inner planet, I'll take note, otherwise I stick to the headlines.

Navigating a horoscope wheel

To begin, let's look in more detail at the information on the horoscope.

Degrees · This little circular symbol ° means degree. The little lines around the wheel represent 1° (one degree) each; zodiac signs are 30° each. The entire wheel is 360°. They help you locate where planets and points are on the chart for precision. The little numbers beside each planet feature this symbol. The number indicates the degree of a planet in a zodiac sign, while the glyph for the sign is next to it so you can see the degree and zodiac sign at a glance. Use these to calculate if a planet is forming an aspect, how strong it is and if it is applying, exact, or separating. Applying means that the planets are moving towards an exact aspect; separating means that the planets are moving away from an exact aspect. If you're great at maths, you'll calculate this visually. If you're a visual/spatial person you'll recognize aspect shapes, and if you're better at reading a list, check out the aspect grid or listing.

Aspect lines · Most horoscopes feature lines between planets that are forming aspects. They may also be colour coded, and feature a tiny glyph for the zodiac sign. They can be challenging to pick out, so check the aspect grid or a list if provided by the program you're using.

Find the ascendant · The ascendant is on the left horizon, marking the beginning of the 1st House. The houses are in sequential order going anti-clockwise through to twelve. While the planets move through the signs, and therefore the chart, anti-clockwise, a live chart moving minute by minute or hour by hour moves clockwise as the signs rise up over the ascendant.

Minute number · On most charts (but not these examples), you'll see another number following the degree number marked like this 21' with a little mark representing minutes – each degree is divided

Aspect grid of transits

March 21, 2023 @ 12:00 pm
Sydney NSW, Australia

Transits

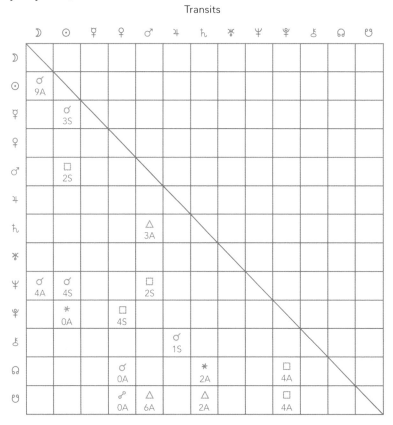

Aspect grid of transits to Charley's birth chart placements

Charley (Claire Howell)

Transits

	☽	☉	☿	♀	♂	♃	♄	♅	♆	♇	⚷	☊	☋
☽	☌ 1S	☍ 2A			△ 0A								☍ 1S
☉		☍ 6S							✶ 2S	△ 3A			
☿									✶ 1A	△ 0S			
♀			△ 0A	☍ 0A					□ 0A		☍ 3S		
♂		□ 4S									△ 3A		
♃							☌ 2A						
♄			☍ 4A	△ 3A						□ 1A	△ 0A		
♅	✶ 3A	△ 7A			☍ 5A	□ 3S						△ 3A	✶ 3A
♆	☌ 5S	☍ 1S			△ 3S				✶ 2A			☍ 5S	☌ 5S
♇		△ 6S		□ 5A			☌ 5A	☌ 2S	✶ 3A	□ 1A			
⚷						✶ 2S	☌ 3A						
☊			△ 1S	☍ 0S					□ 0S		☍ 2A		
☋			✶ 1S	☌ 0S					□ 0S		☌ 2A		

into 60 minutes. So 13° 21′ means 13 degrees and 21 minutes. I've edited out the minutes in these examples. They are useful when calculating a precise time two very slow-moving planets will form an exact aspect to the minute of a degree. However, using the degree is generally all you'll need for now.

Navigating an aspect grid

An aspect grid for a single chart, whether transits, an event or a birth chart, lists planets vertically down one side and then repeated across horizontally at a right angle. Where the lines on the grid intersect between the side and top of the grid shows if there is or isn't an aspect formed between those two planets.

Choose a planet on the aspect grid (page 206), say Neptune, and run your finger across to the right. You can see it is aspecting three planets as there are two conjunction symbols and a square. Run your finger vertically, up from the first aspect and you'll see the Moon is forming the conjunction with Neptune. The second aspect along is a conjunction to the Sun, and the third aspect is a square to Mars.

Looking at the aspect grid for the bi-wheel of these same transits (page 211), this time to Charley's birth chart, we see the symbol for the planets positioned along the left vertical and top horizontal side in the same order once again. This time, however, the left side represents the transiting planets for the time selected, and the top horizontal row of planets represents Charley's natal placements. Go back to T Neptune (on the left of the grid) and you'll see it forms a conjunction (to the N Moon), opposition (to the N Sun), trine (to N Mars) and sextile (to N Neptune).

The aspect grid won't reveal what house position these planets are in or what sign, but you can see the aspects formed. The little number represents the orb or distance they are to an exact aspect, and the little A or S means it's still applying or it's now separating from exact.

Let's read some transits

We'll begin with a transits chart (page 206). Then we'll apply these transits over our example birth chart – the chart on page 211 features the transits chart (outer wheel) around the outside of Charley's birth/natal chart (inner wheel). This double chart is called a bi-wheel.

To understand transits for a general overview of a period, look at the signs and aspects of the outer planets. Don't worry about the house positions for transiting planets unless you're looking at a specific time or event. Stick to planets, aspects and signs.

This transits chart is cast for 21 March 2023, 12pm Sydney, Australia.

To read a transit chart, use the cosmic code: planet + sign, then add in any aspects it's forming, or you can read planet + aspects, then add the sign (and its element and mode).

The collective backdrop – Forecasting over longer timeframes

Neptune · 25° Pisces · Let's begin with Neptune, an outer planet signifying trends in art, spirituality, sensitivity and escapism. Neptune is in Pisces (the sign it rules), which amplifies the themes of spirituality, empathy, diffusion, arts, sensitivity and the pitfall of escapism from life's rougher edges. Look for the Neptune in the chart, symbolized by the little trident/pitchfork glyph.

At 25° of Pisces, we know Neptune has been in this sign for many years (14 years per sign, half a degree per year). By this time, the tells are pervasive throughout the collective as all things mystic, artistic, compassionate and sensitive have mainstreamed. Pisces is a mutable sign and the most likely to dissolve rigid definitions, so we will see diffusion of binary gender roles, identity and sexuality mark this time.

In terms of forecasting into the future, we know in three years from this date Neptune will move into Aries for 14 years. The sign of the times will significantly change; it will be out with unicorns, in with the sacred warrior and an uptick in classic Aries themes.

Work your way around the chart noting sign and degree for

Transits wheel – single wheel

March 21, 2023 @ 12:00 pm
Sydney NSW, Australia

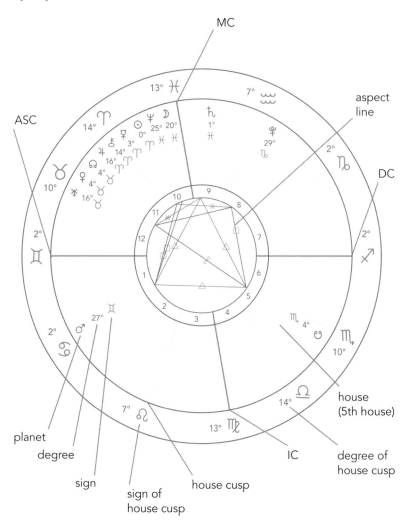

Transits wheel – bi-wheel

Charley
September 16, 1997 @ 9:55pm
Sydney NSW, Australia

Transits
March 21, 2023 @ 12:00 pm
Sydney NSW, Australia

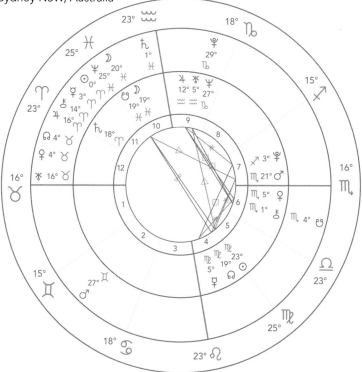

the remaining outer planets. Are they early in a sign, mid or late? This is your major tool for trend prediction, understanding the sign of the times and when it's going to change.

Neptune aspects · Since some outer planets are in a sign for over a decade, look for major aspects to other slow-moving outer planets to signify defining events. These events will push the collective story forward and make sense in context of the bigger picture. In this case, Neptune isn't making any aspects to outer planets. It is, however, forming three aspects, all to faster-moving inner planets. We'll cover this in the next section.

Other outer planets by sign and degree

Chiron · 14° Aries · In this transit chart, Chiron has been in Aries since 2018. Before that, Uranus was in Aries for seven years so Aries themes won't be completely phased out. There's an evolution that will continue around autonomy, independent action and fighting the good fight. Aries in Chiron speaks to wounding around these.

Chiron 14° Aries conjunct Jupiter 16° Aries (separating) · Chiron is making one aspect: a conjunction to Jupiter at 16° Aries. The faster-moving Jupiter is ahead of Chiron by 2°, (technically called an orb of 2°), so the aspect is a separating conjunction; the conjunction has already been exact. A pain point in the collective may erupt around Aries themes and the ongoing theme of this transit of Chiron through Aries. This may be a positive as it could be a reclamation of independence, or it could highlight the need for it. Through the initial pain point, may come healing and a step towards setting something right. Remember the last time Chiron was in Aries (1970s) coincided with 'the battle of the sexes' and civil rights from colour to gender to sexuality, which we're seeing this time around as well.

Uranus · 16° Taurus · Uranus is halfway through Taurus at 16°. Its themes began when it first ingressed into Taurus in 2018, as Greta Thunberg began her humble school strike for climate protest. We know a sign of the times was changing (Uranus into Taurus), so no surprise it captured the zeitgeist and became a movement of millions. We've seen the rise of veganism, leisurewear, destabilizing of economics, the working class and the food industry. Uranus isn't forming any major aspects in this chart.

Pluto · 29° Capricorn, Saturn 1° Pisces · Pluto signals that a change of the guard is coming as it moves into Aquarius in early 2024. Look at Saturn; it's at 1° Pisces, so it's just begun a two and a half-year trek in a new sign, which means it has only just moved out of Aquarius, so those themes have already been introduced: humanitarian, rational, sceptical, abstract and utilitarian. Where Saturn left off, Pluto will deepen and transform, potentially through power struggles, crisis and dismantling in Aquarius-ruled areas. Check last time Pluto was in Aquarius: 1762–1778. As we know, when the guard changes, this is a moment of opportunity that doesn't come along often. How will you make the most of Pluto through Aquarius and ring in the new school? You can be the first cab off the rank, so to speak.

Pluto and Saturn are both forming aspects to faster-moving planets, but not to outer planets.

North node (NN) · 4° Taurus opposite south node (SN) 4° Scorpio (always exact) · The nodes move backwards, so this date is near the end of the north node's journey through Taurus for another 18 years. The NN in Taurus suggests a preference for the tangible over the intangible, metaphysical, taboo or secret. Perhaps a shadow ban on tarot, astrology and modern mystic/witchy-ness since the SN is in Scorpio. A focus on the body, sensuality, food, resources, ecology and natural living continues. The nodes will precess (move backwards through the zodiac) into Aries three months after this point.

The collective – forecasting over short timeframes

Now you know how the long-term astro-weather is based on the signs the outer planets are in and aspects they form to each other. For shorter-term weather, look to faster moving targets, the inner planets, Moon through to Mars.

For a day-to-day forecast, check the Moon by sign and follow

Astro Power

its daily and monthly cycle. Venus, Mercury and Mars move quickly, so follow any major aspects they're making, the mix of signs (elements and modes) and any retrogrades.

Check inner planets for changing astro weather on a daily, weekly or monthly timescale. What's the sign, element and mode balance? Have Mercury, Venus or Mars changed signs recently? When do they change again?

Moon · 20° Pisces conjunct Neptune 25° Pisces (applying) · Let's go back to Neptune at 25° Pisces. On this day, the Moon (indicating the general mood) is also in Pisces. At 20°, it's in orb of a conjunction with Neptune, heightening the themes of Neptune in Pisces as it approaches an exact conjunction in ten hours (with a transit time of two hours per degree).

The distance between Neptune and the Moon is an orb of 4° so it's an applying (or approaching) aspect. Once it moves past the exact conjunction, while still in orb, it's a separating conjunction. Since the Moon completes an orbit every 29.5 days, this aspect occurs monthly. When the Moon meets Neptune in Pisces, the mood is artistic, sensitive and perhaps lost or longing. The perfect time for poetry, music and meditation. Only consider this transit for the mood of the day.

Sun · 0° Aries conjunct Neptune 25° Pisces (separating) · Neptune is also in aspect to the Sun at 0° Aries. While the Sun in Aries is a bold and initiating energy, Neptune's influence means this Aries solar month has a softer start. The Sun rules identity, so this is still tied up with Neptune's themes of compassion, art and escape. Perhaps it's a sleepier beginning, energy may be diffuse or groggy, and the life force, identity and focus are less individualistic. The spiritual warrior is a theme with this sign combo.

Mars · 27° Gemini square Neptune 25° Pisces (separating) · Mars at 27° Gemini is forming a square aspect to Neptune. It's a tight orb which makes it strong, although this is a waxing square, so Mars has already moved past the exact square by 2°. Neptune square to Mars suggests hidden motives, action or confusion around the right action or path. Perhaps acting on data is at cross purposes with empathy or intuition, so watch for a contradiction here. This could be quite a passive-aggressive influence, so over these few days you'd keep that in mind. This could be a low-energy time as Neptune, as the outer planet, dissipates the energy and direction of Mars.

Continue through the personal planets looking at the Sun through to Mars, noting the signs and aspects for each. Inner planets in aspect to each other, for example the Sun square Mars, are quick moving so have less impact than outer planet to outer planet, or inner planet to outer planet. However, they're useful for planning, conversation, observation, sharing your astro-forecast on socials, or writing horoscopes, as they change so often.

Your destiny – transits to your birth chart

Your birth chart already holds the keys to your destiny, however, transits are like timers and markers. They reveal what will be activated, when and how easy or challenging the change might be. To read the transits to a birth/natal chart, it's time to step up your cosmic code-breaking, so we'll start to use shorthand:
T is for transiting planets, N is for Natal planet placements.

Cosmic code

T Planet + N house + aspects from T planet to N planets:
- Identify the T planet.
- What sign is the T planet in?
- Which house in the birth chart is the T planet in?
- When the transit chart is overlayed around the natal chart in a bi-wheel you'll see which natal house the transiting planet is in, or in this case, overlayed onto.

Aspects

- Is the transiting planet making any aspects to natal planets? Or to natal points like the Asc, IC, DC or MC?
- How close are the orbs?
- Is the aspect applying, exact or separating?
- What is the timeframe of this aspect if it's a major one?
- When did it begin, when is it at maximum influence (exact) and when will it be out of range/over?

Here we go, astro-mystics!

For this example, we're overlaying the transits chart (outer wheel) over a natal chart (inner wheel), so it's time to apply the themes we already looked at in context of the collective, and ground it down into a unique natal chart, as well as living experience.

As mentioned for the natal chart example, we're using Charley's chart, which is the same one used in my book *Star Power*. To learn how to interpret a birth chart, pick up a copy.

If an outer planet isn't forming an aspect to a personal planet or major point (Asc, IC, DC, MC), interpret its meaning for the house it's transiting in. In this case interpret it for this area of your life.

To begin you can come up with a formula, or just see what stands out to you and begin there. There's no right or wrong way.

T Uranus 16° Taurus conjunct N Asc 16 ° Taurus (exact) · For the transits to Charley's chart, I see an outer planet (Uranus) is exactly conjunct Charley's ASC. That's a big deal as it's outer, and on the ASC which, if you've ever experienced this transit, can't be ignored. Since Charley's ASC is 16° Taurus, the themes of Uranus in Taurus have been around for years so they're not new and Charley will have already adjusted to them. As Uranus has spent this portion of its time in Taurus, transiting through her 12th House up until this point, Charley will have been percolating somewhat. Now she's ready to express or become conscious of what those themes are. Uranus is sudden, destabilizing and progressive.

Applied to the N ASC it may mean a sudden burst of energy, drastic change in direction, outlook or look. Charley represents the zeitgeist and feels personally in tune with the progressive side of culture. She may be part of bringing in change, new ideas or progress culture in some way. This is a radical re-invention and suggests exciting times ahead. If ever there was a time to change her look or go for a shock value, this is it. For a music artist, this transit will be a wild ride Charley is well positioned to benefit from since they work in the creative space. Someone that relies on a stable and conservative persona would find it much more challenging as it so often suggests extreme lane changes.

T NN Taurus in Natal 12th House | T SN Scorpio conjunct Venus in 6th House · Another close connection is the T SN conjunct N Venus. It's an applying conjunction with an orb of 1°. Relationships aren't the focus for this time. Due to the T NN in the 12th House, over this period, Charley will benefit from time in solitude whether that's creative, spiritual or rest and relaxation.

T Saturn in N 10th House · This is the *your star has risen* signature. At this point, Charley should have hit a high point in her career, with opportunity to establish herself. Since she has indeed been working towards her goals as a music artist over the years leading up to this point, I expect this transit to be rewarding. At this point it's imperative she builds on whatever success she gains, securing herself by making decisions for the long term. Since Saturn has just moved into Pisces (it's at 1°) music and arts are favoured professionally. Charley has N Moon in Pisces in this House, so fortune will smile on her emotional style. It's time to truly sing her heart out.

Other themes of Pisces are jewellery, idealized beauty and even film. Perhaps Charley will get a shot at one or more of these areas. Pisces is a mutable sign, so can multi-hyphen life, in this case, professionally. Once Saturn conjuncts Charley's Moon, these opportunities may catalyze. The pitfall, however, is that a lot of work leaves less time for emotional connection and needs. The saying, 'it's lonely at the top', might describe this period. Saturn conjunct the Moon tends to coincide with feeling a little lonely or isolated. If you're ready to graft, however, Saturn is there for you!

T Neptune in the 10th House, conjunct the Moon and SN (separating) · Let's look at T Neptune in relation to the natal chart. It's also in the 10th House, however, it's much further along than T Saturn so at Neptune's snail's pace we know it's been there for years. This is a mystical planet so responding to this archetype in the career zone has been in line with Charley's dual creative professions as a make-up artist and a music artist over this period. T Neptune is still in a separating orb of her Natal Moon and SN. Song lyrics came to her in dreams, which she wrote down on waking. Her songs are emotional and a way to channel her feelings around a heart break and lost love. Disappointment, longing and loss can be a pitfall of Neptune with its function of dissolution, however, turning the experience into art is also on brand and a functional way to serve the deity while it has set up its temple in the career zone.

The question, 'is it good or is it bad?', depends on perspective since, like most things, it's everything at once. Neptune in aspect to a personal planet, especially the Sun, Moon or Venus, may coincide with surrendering that part of oneself to a higher cause or a higher power. In this case, through her career, Charley is sharing her most painful feelings in a way others can relate to. Over this period she has been signed to EMI as a recording artist, released singles and was a finalist to represent Australia for the Eurovision song contest. The 10th is a house of fame, as well as reputation. It's highly visible. By responding to the siren call of Neptune in her career, Charley looks to benefit. At the same time, one could say, Charley's success so far is easily predicted due to this transit. The hands of the cosmic clock coincide with external and internal events once again.

T Moon 20° Pisces conjunct N Moon/SN, opposite N Sun/NN · Looking at faster-moving planets, the T Moon is in Pisces conjunct Charley's N Moon, so it's a lunar return. Charley will resonate with the emotional temperature and mood, and perhaps be drawn to connect with her fanbase on social media to fulfil her own emotional needs. Opposite the Sun suggests it's important Charley leans into her emotional and instinctual life for balance, letting things flow, not getting caught up in Virgo detail or definitions, especially at home or with family. It's not a cleaning day, Virgo!

T Venus is in Charley's 12th House, doubling up on finding flow, escapism, as well as channelling the collective through creativity.

These are some examples to get you rolling. Work your way through Charley's chart as practice or go straight onto your own, those of people you know and love, as well as people in the spotlight if that's your groove.

Create a timeline

Write out a timeline of the biggest events in your life (including inner events) to keep handy so you can compare it as you track back over your transits. Run through any big transits from outer planets, especially to your Sun, Moon, Venus and Asc and note down the dates in a timeline. Then compare the two. What were the major destiny points where events and astrology correlated? Can you see the deeper archetypes at play here? Does the scenario make more sense armed with your astrological perspective? Can you see other ways you might have responded more consciously, or do you feel you met your destiny and it was meant to be?

Next, track ahead to what's coming up and create a timeline of the headline transits to your natal chart, as well as a timeline with the faster-moving transits so you can observe how they express and the quality or feel they have. Keep a basic diary so you can look back and track cycles.

Always remember, your inner compass is one of your most precious assets, while astrology is an excellent tool or framework to facilitate, focus and structure it. Your destiny isn't just waiting, it's calling you to make the most of your unique path and precious life. Give it your all by navigating towards your North Star, forging your own path, teaming up with people that share and mutually amplify your best life.

Resources / Partial bibliography

SOURCE MATERIAL FROM

Astro*Synthesis course notes
Second year course notes from Stella Woods (aka Starwoman)
Second year applied astrology
Tony Howard and Steven Forrest on Planets OOB
Chiron and The Healing Journey by Melanie Reinhart
Christopher Renstrom lecture 'Does Uranus Make me Gay?'
Venus and Aphrodite, A Biography of Desire by Bethany Hughes
Women and Power, a Manifesto by Mary Beard

GET A PRO READING

with Vanessa Montgomery by scheduling at **AstroAllStarz.com**

ASTROLOGICAL RESOURCES

Astrological Aspects, A Process-Oriented Approach by Leyla Rael
    and Dane Rudhyar
Astrology, Karma and Transformation by Stephen Arroyo
The Changing Sky by Steven Forrest
The Combination of Stellar Influences by Reinhold Ebertin
Cosmos and Psyche by Richard Tarnas
The Gods of Change by Howard Sassportas
Predictive Astrology the Eagle and the Lark by Bernadette Brady
Retrograde Planets by Erin Sullivan

Other books by all of the above plus Liz Greene, Demetra George,
    Brian Clark, Melanie Reinhart, Jessica Lanyadoo, Chani Nicholas

FIND WHERE THE PLANETS ARE NOW
(+ make your birth chart | free + paid)

Astroallstarz.com – make a chart, clear list of all placements
Astro.com – make a chart, including asteroids + bonus resources
AstrologyForDays.com – month by month online interactive
  calendar of transits – subscription $ (use the code
  ASTROALLSTARZ at the checkout to get a discount)
AstroGold.io – birth and transit charts – one-time payment $$
LUNAastrology.com – birth and transit charts – budget subscription
  $ (use the code **ASTROALLSTARZ** at the checkout to get a
  discount)
Solar Fire – esotech.com.au – comprehensive pro program. One-
  time payment $$$
Time Passages – astrograph.com – one-time payment $$

ASTRO ANNUAL PLANNER/DIARY
(northern + southern)

Magicofi.com – beautiful, bonus material, general transits, lunations
  (use the code **ASTROALLSTARZ** at the checkout to get a
  discount)
Honeycomb.co – annual almanac/planner, includes your
  personalized transits and birth chart

STUDY PRO ASTROLOGY

AstroSynthesis.com.au – downloadable course units in audio and
  PDF
Astrologyuniversity.com – participate live or download later + a la
  cart webinars and workshops

Contact the official governing body in your country for
  recommended schools, courses, group meetings etc:

USA – **astrologers.com**
UK – **professionalastrologers.co.uk**
Australia – **faainc.org.au**

TRACE THE MYTHS

The Knot of Time, Astrology and Female Experience by Lindsay
  River and Sally Gillespie
Pandora's Jar, Women in the Greek Myths by Natalie Haynes
Symbols for Women, a Feminist Guide to the Zodiac by Sheila
  Farrant

Also, learn from legendary herstorians Bethany Hughes, Mary
  Beard, Natalie Haynes, Kara Cooney, Silvia Federici, Safron Rossi
  and Marija Gimbutus.

Acknowledgements

Thank you, dear reader, for investigating astrology, mythology and enchanting the world as a modern mystic. May you always follow your inner guidance and co-create your destiny with the cosmos.

Thank you to Charley for sharing your birth chart, transits and story for the how-to chapter example. Keep up with Charley's journey at www.itmecharley.com to see how the transits unfold.

Thank you to everyone who has had a hand in creating, supporting, retailing, promoting and sharing *Astro Power*. Harriet Webster, thank you for commissioning and guiding *Astro Power* into the world. You are amazing! A cool, calm, gracious professional, it's been a pleasure to work with you once again. Thank you, Wendy Hobson, for editing my writing from tome to wonderful handbook. Original commissioning editor Zena Alkayat, thank you for finding me and kicking off the Power series with *Star Power* – and now your own Bloom empire, our gardens are growing! Thanks goes to Giulia for your beautiful design, layout and illustrations. This book wouldn't be all it could without your interpretation. Thank you to everyone at Quadrille Publishing and Hardie Grant for continuing the astro-journey and producing such quality work.

Thank you to my friends who have been so patient with my absence, my Brisbane girl gang, Melbourne family who I miss so much, Nadine Maloney for continuing to furnish Melbourne friends and family with the gift of astrology! Thank you to Lyndal Walker for being the Gemini, proofreading, feedback and generally being my modern messenger. Thank you to Fiona and Chet Howell for your patience and providing private studio space to work from.

Thanks once again to my sterling astrology foundation, Glennys Lawton and Brian Clark of Astro*synthesis and Stella Woods (aka Stella Starwoman); my wonderful teachers who have equipped me to develop and pass on this knowledge. Also, thanks to the stellar firmament of people flexing astrology, Tony Howard, Jessica Lanyadoo and Chani Nichols for solid contributions to the field.

MANAGING DIRECTOR Sarah Lavelle
COMMISSIONING EDITOR Harriet Webster
EDITOR Wendy Hobson
DESIGN AND ILLUSTRATION Giulia Garbin
HEAD OF PRODUCTION Stephen Lang
PRODUCTION CONTROLLER Sabenna Atchia

Published in 2022 by Quadrille,
an imprint of Hardie Grant Publishing

Quadrille
52–54 Southwark Street
London SE1 1UN
quadrille.com

ISBN 978 1 78713 889 6

Printed in China